Just Say No

For Parents, Grandparents, Aunts, and Uncles

Also by Garrett K. Scanlon

Seeing Past Friday Night

A Road to Bountiful

Walking and Talking

Single Page Life Plan

Just Say No

For Parents, Grandparents, Aunts, and Uncles

BECAUSE EVERY HERO NEEDS A GUIDE

A Powerful Plan to Help Your Teen Confront Drugs, Alcohol, and Tobacco in High School

GARRETT K. SCANLON
Author of *Seeing Past Friday Night*

JustSayNo.org

BALLYLONGFORD BOOKS

Copyright © 2017 by Garrett K. Scanlon

JustSayNo.org
250 Civic Center Dr. 5th Floor CASTO
Columbus, OH 43215

All rights reserved. No part of this book may be reproduced in any manner or form whatsoever, by any means, electronically or mechanically, including photocopying or recording, or by any information or retrieval system, or in relation to goods and/or seminars (including seminars, workshops, training programs, classes, etc.) without the expressed, written permission from the publisher, except by a reviewer, who may quote brief passages for reviews or articles about the book.

Disclaimer: The author of this publication is not an attorney and the reader should not consider the information contained herein to be legal advice. The draftsman of the Just Say No Promise Agreement at the end of this book is not an attorney and this agreement is not, and is not intended to be, a legally enforceable contract, but merely an aid for young adults and their sponsors. Reader shall hold Garrett Scanlon harmless from any and all claims, lawsuits, demands, causes of action, liability, loss, damage and/or injury, of any kind. If the reader wants to create an enforceable contract, he or she should consult an attorney.

Names: Scanlon, Garrett K., author.

Title: Just say no for parents, grandparents, aunts, and uncles because every story needs a hero : a powerful plan to help your teen confront drugs, alcohol, and tobacco in high school / Garrett K. Scanlon.

Description: First edition. | Columbus, OH : Ballylongford Books, [2017]

Identifiers: ISBN: 978-0-9961943-1-0 (softcover) | 978-0-9961943-3-4 (eBook) | LCCN: 2017943397

Subjects: LCSH: Parent and teenager—Handbooks, manuals, etc. | Grandparents—Handbooks, manuals, etc. | Aunts—Handbooks, manuals, etc. | Uncles—Handbooks, manuals, etc. | Teenagers—United States—Conduct of life. | High school students—Conduct of life. | Peer pressure in adolescence—United States. | Teenagers—Drug use—United States—Prevention. | Teenagers—Alcohol use—United States—Prevention. | Teenagers—Tobacco use—United States—Prevention. | BISAC: FAMILY & RELATIONSHIPS / Life Stages / Teenagers.

Classification: LCC: HQ799.15 .S33 2017 | DDC: 306.874—dc23

Printed and bound in the United States of America.
First printing 2017. Excerpts are available for reprinting in your publication.

Author is available to speak at your elementary school, middle school, high school, parent group, Rotary, PSR group, church group, and drug and alcohol prevention events.

Visit www.JustSayNo.org

Cover image courtesy of iStockphoto.com
Front cover design: Kristine Coplin
Text design: by www.tothepointsolutions.com

*Dedicated to you,
the parents, grandparents, aunts, and uncles who ...*

Fight the good fight against the challenges teens face every day.

Help your teen dream heroic dreams.

Understand that a teenager's life can be tough, but becomes infinitely easier when they set rational boundaries on their own behavior to achieve long-term goals.

Are willing to provide added incentives for the young adults in your life to make good decisions and overcome the influences of binge drinking, drug use, and smoking!

This book is dedicated to you, the guide!

CONTENTS

Introduction for Parents — 9

1. "Attention Parents! Your Teen Has Just Left the Village." — 15
2. "They Just Aren't Thinking." — 19
3. Every Story Needs a Guide — 25
4. Aunts, Uncles, and TuTu Kane! Valuable Allies — 29
5. The *Just Say No* Promise Agreement — 33
6. Standing Up to Beer Pressure — 37
7. You Don't Expect This to Actually Work, Do You? — 39
8. 10 Questions About the *Just Say No* Plan — 45
9. What is the Most Dangerous Substance for Your Teen? — 51
10. The Power of *Just Saying No* — 53
11. Uh Oh … We Didn't Think of Everything — 55
12. 11 More Things You Can Do to Keep Your Teen Safe — 59
13. Types of Incentives and Rewards — 63

Afterword for Parents, Grandparents, Aunts, and Uncles — 67

How to Bring *Just Say No* to Your Group — 68

PART TWO

Just Say No Because Every Story Needs a Hero

Includes a Promise Agreement to Earn Added Rewards for Saying No to Binge Drinking, Drug Use, and Smoking in High School

	A Letter to You	77
1.	Every Story Needs a Hero	81
2.	You Have the Right to Dream Heroic Dreams	85
3.	A Collision Course	89
4.	How I Got the Use of a Car	91
5.	Seeing Past Friday Night	93
6.	And He's My Friend!	95
7.	The Power of Saying No	97
8.	The Great Paradox	99
9.	Incentives and Rewards: The *Just Say No* Promise Agreement	103
10.	Free Samples and Other Sales Tactics	107
11.	How to Prepare for Your Polygraph	111
12.	"What in the World Does Someone Like Me Have to Look Forward To?"	113
13.	Finding Your Guitar	117
14.	The Two Imposters—Triumph and Disaster	121
15.	"I Wish I Had Smoked More Cigarettes."	125
16.	A Letter to Your Future Self	127
	Thank You!	129
	About the Author	131
	Just Say No Agreement with Rewards	133
	Just Say No Agreement—No Rewards	135

INTRODUCTION FOR PARENTS

Because of a flexible schedule that comes from a career in investment real estate, and two kids who were going through middle school, I became a volunteer instructor for Junior Achievement of Central Ohio. It is a very rewarding, and humbling experience.

I was always very comfortable speaking to business groups, but getting in front of a group of young teens for the first time—now *that* was pressure! We discussed such topics as how to interview for a job, why to avoid credit card debt, and yes, why real estate is a great investment. It was heartening to hear these kids talk about the lofty dreams and aspirations they had for their future.

But, it soon became apparent that these young teens face a storm that looms right around the corner; a storm that threatens every dream they have.

A War on Our Kids: Our kids are living in a drug-saturated world where heroin is readily available, all day long, for the cost of a large pizza. In response:

Some say we should *ramp up our war* on drugs.

Others believe that we should *end our war* on drugs.

What war? Drug overdoses are at an all-time high, teens continue to get hooked on cigarettes, and binge drinking among young adults is pervasive. The only war has been on our teens.

The suppliers are on one side. You, the parents, grandparents, aunts, and uncles are on the other.

The Suppliers:
- Have a sophisticated distribution system,
- Are relentless in the promotion of their products,
- Rarely pay taxes, and
- Are glamorized by Hollywood.

You on the other hand:
- Work crazy hours,
- Pay a lot of taxes, and the last time we checked,
- Are *not* glamorized by Hollywood.

SO, HOW DO YOU PROTECT YOUR TEENS? HOW DO YOU PROTECT YOUR FAMILY?

These are the questions I began to ask myself as I looked out at the classrooms full of students who were about to begin their high school years, or who were already freshmen and sophomores. Soon they would be making crucial decisions regarding drugs, alcohol, and tobacco that threatened to obliterate every goal they had. So, I began discussing ways they could effectively confront this serious danger they were about to face.

As the war on our teens continued to escalate, I provided them with powerful concepts and tangible tools to help them safely navigate their upcoming high school years; to help them *See Past Friday Night* (the title of my first book on this subject); to avoid the severe consequences of bad decisions; to help them *just get through those years safely*!

This resulted in the **Just Say No Plan**.

Recently, I asked a group of 30 eighth-graders, "How many of you are familiar with the slogan, *Just Do It*?"

As you can imagine, every single student raised their hand. The slogan has become one of the most powerful mission statements in the world for Nike. Don't just *say* you're going to run that marathon, don't just *say* you're going to climb that mountain ... *Just do it!* There is no need to endlessly explain your motivations, or to make excuses, or to get ready to get ready ... *Just do it!*

SIMPLE. NOT *EASY*, BUT *SIMPLE*.

Then I asked them another question. "How many of you have heard of the strategy to *Just Say No*?" Not a single hand went up. Blank expressions all around for what was once a powerful rallying cry for teens across America, Canada, and Europe. Times have changed.

When you and I were in school:
- Pot was the cheapest, most available drug.
- The level of THC, the chemical found in pot, was around 3.5%.
- There was a stigma attached to cocaine.
- High school kids had an intense fear of heroin.
- DWI's, DUI's, OVI's, and OWI's were not all that common.
- Breathalyzer limits were relatively high.
- Police officers were as likely to follow you home, or let you call your parents, as they were to arrest you.
- Embarrassing behavior was not posted on social media.

Your teen's world is entirely different:
- The THC level of pot hovers around 10-12%.
- Heroin is the most available drug.
- Heroin is one of the *cheapest* drugs.
- The stigma and fear of using heavy drugs is much less.

- DWI's, and the other 'I's', are very common and extremely expensive.
- Your teens cannot expect a courtesy 'follow-home' by police.
- Your child's behavior is posted online for all the world to see.

DIFFERENT TIMES CALL FOR DIFFERENT MEASURES.

It is time to arm your teen with a proven plan to fight this storm; to *Just Say No*.

- It helps them make their decision *before* 'the ask'.
- It puts them in control.
- It gives them added incentives to stay strong.
- It is a plan that works, even when they stumble, if they stumble.
- It gives them a great *excuse* to say no.
- It's simple. No need for them to continually debate their decision.

There are two parts to *Just Say No for Parents, Grandparents, Aunts, and Uncles*.

Part 1: Explains the *Just Say No Plan* to you, the *guide* of a high school student:

- How to help your teen transition from a young teenager to a responsible young adult,
- Why it is important to keep things simple,
- A big reason why some teens try drugs in the first place,
- Why your teen has the right to dream heroic dreams,

INTRODUCTION FOR PARENTS

- The Promise Agreement you and your teen will sign,
- 10 Questions parents have about the *Just Say No Plan*,
- What to do if there is a stumble,
- Examples of incentives you can offer.

Part 2: The second part of this book is an exact replica of the book, *Just Say No—Because Every Story Needs a Hero*, that your son or daughter should read. Included is a *Just Say No* Promise Agreement for the teen and his or her parent, grandparent, aunt, or uncle, that can be personalized to your particular circumstance.

The war on drugs, alcohol, and tobacco does not *end* with your kids. It *begins* with them. It *begins* with you. Together, you are on the front line!

So, let's get started ...

CHAPTER 1

"Attention Parents! Your Teen Has Just Left the Village."

It may have been the best-planned social event that my wife and I ever attended … 8th Grade Graduation for our daughter and her 57 classmates! Months of intense preparation by a 12-parent committee resulted in an impressive graduation ceremony followed by a dinner party that culminated in a professionally edited music video featuring photographs and video clips of the kids as they surfed through 8 years of:

- Classroom activity and spelling bees,
- Track events and swimming meets,
- Class trips and birthday parties,
- Trips to museums and zoos,
- Summer vacations and volunteer projects,
- Science fairs and talent competitions, and
- All of those travel teams!

I thought, "Wow. *It really does take a village to raise a child*." Like my wife and I, you were undoubtedly an important part of that village consisting of parents, teachers, coaches, doctors, educators, grandparents, aunts, uncles, and of course, babysitters. Together, we were like a well-oiled machine! Then, something rather earth shattering occurred. The kids were sent off to a place called *High School*.

"WHO?"

Up until that point, we knew all of her friends and had formed many friendships with their parents. We coached them in sports and volunteered in the cafeteria. We carpooled them everywhere and knew all of their teachers and coaches.

In high school, however, there was an entirely new set of teachers, coaches, and friends who we had never met before. My wife and I would ask her, "Now, **Who** is that again?" and "You're going to **Who's** house?" and "**Who's** driving?"

Usually, we never even found out who **Who** was!

Our teen had left the village. Ready or not, she was becoming a young adult. We had raised a child with the help of a village. Now it was time to help her transition into a strong individual; a responsible adult.

IT REALLY DOES TAKE A STRONG INDIVIDUAL TO BECOME A RESPONSIBLE ADULT:

All of a sudden, she was in a different world; one that wasn't particularly excited about receiving parental help and input. And, quite frankly, we didn't have the time and energy to start all over again for her four short years of high school. But, we were concerned about having her navigate this new world by herself.

She was about to make new friends, learn to drive a 1,500-lb car 65 miles per hour down the freeway on snowy nights, and say either yes or no to binge-drinking, smoking, and drug use. She would begin new activities and make new decisions that would have enormous consequences that would extend well into her future. She was on the verge of receiving an explosion of new freedoms and independence at a time when her level of experience in these matters was relatively low. The village that we knew so well was gone. And, we knew very little of her new world.

All of a sudden, we had to rely on her to make big, important decisions when we were not around. While we felt she was prepared, we still found it to be a bit scary. Maybe you have felt the same way.

THE BOTTOM LINE IS THIS:

On Friday night, when your son or daughter finds out that they didn't ...

- Make the basketball team, or
- Pass that chemistry exam you told them they better ace, or
- Get that part in the play they so desperately wanted, or
- Anticipate that 'break-up' text from their girlfriend or boyfriend.

And someone comes up to them and says, "Who cares? Let's go get high."

When this happens, their teachers will not be there. The police will not be there. Their coaches will not be there. You will not be there.

THE GOOD NEWS IS …

- No matter **where** your teen is,
- No matter **what time of day or night** it is,

- No matter **how often** he or she has to make a critical decision,

There is one person who will always be there. *Your teen!* Wherever your son or daughter goes, he or she is always there! **The one person who can *Just Say No*.**

This can seem daunting, that they are relying on themselves. But, it is also *liberating* for them. Personal responsibility *empowers* them! Rather than rely on the police, homeland security, or a dozen unknown forces out there, they can be the hero that keeps them and their siblings safe. It is your job to guide them to be their own hero; to provide them a safe path for their journey.

Your teen has to transition from the village, to their new world … fast!

CHAPTER 2

"They Just Aren't Thinking."

Across the table, with coffee in hand, the police sergeant patiently answered all of my questions. A graduate of Notre Dame, he had been involved in thousands of drug encounters during an exceptional career that spanned three decades with the Columbus Division of Police. He was the perfect person to shed light on the growing problem of drug use among high school students, and I was eager to learn as much as possible from him for my book, *Seeing Past Friday Night*.

THE FUNDAMENTAL QUESTION

After a lengthy conversation, I asked a final question that he was uniquely qualified to answer. I wanted to know the main reason why a teen tries drugs for the very first time. A lot of different reasons are typically cited, including everything from improving academic performance, to fitting in, losing weight, wanting to party, and mimicking some of their parent's behavior. Every teen can find a reason to partake, but obviously, not all of them do. So, is there a more universal, overriding reason?

"You've witnessed it all," I said. "You've seen the destruction, the incredible cost. You're the person who explains to the parents why their child was arrested. So, the question is, when some kids try drugs for the first time, what is the overriding reason?"

"I don't know," he said. "*They* don't know. They just say they weren't thinking."

"Okay, I get that," I responded. "But, when you really think about it … what is the main cause?"

This time he took longer and said, "It's really hard to say. I can tell you what the parent's reaction is, every single time."

"What's that?"

"Absolute shock. When I tell them that their 16 or 17 year old son or daughter was just arrested for selling drugs to support their own habit, they are absolutely shocked. They can't believe it, which, of course, is understandable."

His words made me recall how many times parents say, "I gotta tell you, I would be absolutely shocked to find out that any of my kids were doing drugs." The sergeant's sobering words made me realize that just because parents would be *absolutely shocked* that their kids would try drugs, this does not necessarily eliminate the possibility.

PRESSING ON WITH THE FUNDAMENTAL QUESTION …

Apologizing for being stuck on this one question, I asked a third time.

"Think about it. You've seen so many great kids from wonderful families go down a dangerous path during their high school years. In many cases, if they could only go back in time and change that one decision, their whole life might be very different."

He pondered one more time, and after a long moment, shook his head and said, "They all say the same thing. They just weren't thinking."

That's when it finally struck me ...

THAT *IS* THE ANSWER. THEY *DON'T* DECIDE ... THEY *REACT*!

"That's it," I said. "We're searching for the answer, and that is the answer. They aren't taking the time to create a list with the *pros* on one side of the page and the *cons* on the other. They don't decide ... they react!"

THERE *IS* NO *REASON* FOR THEIR DECISION, BECAUSE THERE ISN'T MUCH *REASONING* INVOLVED.

Like so many things we do, particularly in high school when our experience level is so disproportionate to the consequences of our decisions, we just react. This is one of the reasons why signing a *Just Say No* Promise Agreement has proven to be so successful.

The thinking is done in advance.

They *Just Say No*. They don't:
- Debate it,
- Defend their position,
- Continually fight peer pressure and justify their decision.

They just react. They *Just Say No*.

The decision is made in advance, when cooler heads prevail!

HOW WOULD YOU ANSWER?

Imagine that you're at a big event at a school that is being covered by the local media. A young schoolgirl raises her hand and asks you, "What should we do if someone offers us drugs?"

Cameras are rolling. Microphones are pointed at you. Teachers and other parents are looking your way. What are you going to say?

In earlier days, I probably would have answered, "Well, tell them that drugs are bad for you. Your grades will suffer. Your parents don't want you to do it. It's illegal. Oh, and tell them ..."

Blah, blah, blah.

The girl doesn't need a Ben Franklin sheet with talking points to carry around with her! She needs to be armed with a **simple, powerful mission statement**. A mission statement that *she* is in charge of implementing! Isn't that *exactly* what every sports brand does, whether selling athletic apparel, basketball shoes, or sports beverages? Their slogan is a simple, powerful mission statement.

The very best advice you can give her is to *Just Say No*.

Not, **no because of this**.

Not, **no because of that**.

No, because I said so!

She doesn't have to explain herself to anybody! Just Saying No, is enough.

If your kids are going to 'react', have them react in a positive way.

WHY I *JUST SAID NO* IN HIGH SCHOOL

Despite a long list of ill-advised things I probably did in high school, using drugs, alcohol, and tobacco was not one of them. Why?

Because my parents offered me an agreement with added incentives to *Just Say No*:
- They gave me use of a car,
- They paid for some of the gasoline and car insurance, and
- They offered me a monthly allowance.

After that, it was always a *beer* or a *car*, a *cigarette* or a *car*, *pot* or a *car*. At 16, 17, and 18, *car* wins out every time. Decision made. From that moment on, I never thought about it. From that point on, I *reacted* in a positive way. It was reflexive.

AN AGREEMENT FOR YOUR OWN SON, DAUGHTER, GRANDCHILD, NIECE, OR NEPHEW

The concepts, strategies, and Promise Agreement in this book were developed from my years in the classroom as a volunteer counselor, my personal high school experience, and from conversations with teachers, coaches, psychiatrists, addiction experts, police officers, and other parents.

Empower your daughter or son with a mission statement that is:
- **Simple,**
- **Powerful, and**
- **Achievable**

A mission statement that:
- **Motivates them wherever they go,**
- **Gives them a tangible excuse to use against peer pressure,**
- ***They* are in charge of implementing!**

This is role you play as a parent, because every story needs a guide ...

CHAPTER 3

Every Story Needs a Guide

Any novelist, screenwriter, or playwright will tell you that every story needs **a hero**. The hero is on **a journey**. Then, **a crisis** occurs; an enormous threat or challenge that the hero must defeat or overcome.

Out of a cast of characters, emerges **a guide**; an ally that comes alongside to help the hero. There are **high stakes** involved, and **a plan of action** that will result in a **resolute outcome**.

For a story to resonate with us, it must have these elements. Because, that's life!

- **A Hero**
- **A Journey**
- **A Crisis or Threat**
- **A Guide**
- **High Stakes**
- **A Plan of Action**
- **A Resolute Outcome**

In this true-life story, your son or daughter is the hero. They might not *think* they are a hero, because heroes do not always *feel* particularly heroic during their high school years. They are not yet aware of the super-powers they possess. Eventually, they will discover they have super-powers that are perfectly suited for a big future. But, those powers don't always apply to what is important to your teen *right now*.

Some of their greatest skills and abilities that will help them become a great novelist, or entrepreneur, or firefighter, or nurse, or chef, or teacher, or Army Ranger, or songwriter are usually unrelated to scoring touchdowns or starring in the school play. It's hard for you to tell your teenager, "Don't worry about that. Your day will come." But what William Shakespeare once wrote, is particularly true for teens today: *We know what we are, but not what we may be.*

The Hero: Regardless of any limitations or challenges they might have, your daughter or son is designed for greatness. They have the right to dream heroic dreams.

The Journey: They are on a *crucial* journey in high school, with a cast of characters that includes new friends, teachers, and coaches.

They have to deal with changing physiology, peer pressure, and the emotional swings that occur when they get their driver's license one day, and get cut from the soccer team the next.

The Crisis/Threat: A storm is coming. A storm that leaves a potential path of incredible destruction. The single biggest threat to your teen living a powerful life is him or her making a bad decision regarding the use of drugs, alcohol, and tobacco.

The Guide: *You*, the parents, are the guides! If they are Rocky Balboa, then you are his trusted fight-trainer, Mickey, who prepared him to survive all 15 rounds. You have to help *your* fighter get through all 4 years!

Other guides include their grandparents, aunts, and uncles who can also help them *Just Say No*.

High Stakes: At stake for your teen, is a loss of respect, DWI's/DUI's/OWI's, lawyer fees, suffering grades, loss of car privileges, addiction, team expulsions, and a risk that their siblings will follow suit.

The Plan of Action (The Promise Agreement): In the back of this book is a win-win *Just Say No* Promise Agreement for you and your teen that spells out the terms and conditions required for your teen to receive added rewards. There is a second Promise Agreement that does not include rewards.

This Story's Resolute Outcome: Rewards begin immediately and victory comes at graduation when you and the hero shake hands on a job well done. Your reward is seeing your hero, your son or daughter, become the best version of themselves. The stakes are high.

We root for the hero. We root for the guide. We root for *you*!

Are you up for the challenge?

CHAPTER 4

AUNTS, UNCLES, AND TUTU KANE! VALUABLE ALLIES

Some of the most successful and meaningful *Just Say No* Promise Agreements have been between aunts and uncles and their nieces and nephews.

THERE IS A REASON FOR THIS

This is because sometimes a teen will rationalize breaking a rule with the idea that it is natural for a parent and a teen to battle each other over such things. Besides, they see their friends breaking rules, set by their parents, all the time. They might also rationalize that some of the rewards and incentives they receive for *just saying no* are things that their friends get *for free*!

Karen's parents pay for her cell phone and they give her a huge allowance, and she doesn't have to promise to do the same things I do.

My parents should be giving me these things anyway!

ULTERIOR MOTIVES!

Teens might also suspect that there are ulterior motives at play.

- *They are trying to manipulate me.*
- *They just keep wanting to control everything I do!*
- *They can't stop telling me how to live my life.*
- *They just can't relate to my generation.*

Right or wrong, many of us had these same thoughts when we were teens.

BUT, IT'S JUST DIFFERENT WITH AUNTS AND UNCLES

With an aunt or an uncle (or even a grandparent) it is an entirely different thing. The teen *knows* that the incentives being provided by an aunt or uncle is not their responsibility. They recognize that it is a genuine sacrifice. And, they don't see many of their friend's extended family going to the expense of offering added perks and rewards for *Just Saying No*. The teens truly know that their aunt, uncle, or grandparents are acting out of love, with no designs other than to help them succeed.

And the relationship with an aunt or an uncle is just different for a teen, than it is with their parents. Teens often confide in a different way with their aunts and uncles. Teens are oftentimes more willing to listen to them with more of an open mind than they are with their parents. And, aunts and uncles are sometimes able to communicate in a more direct and candid way than a parent can.

A friend of mine, who is the aunt of three nephews, once said, "I think the boys listen to me differently than they do my brother and sister-in-law because they know that any advice I give them is solely based on the love I have for them. With me, they know they are getting unfiltered advice. I am sure there are times when the message I am giving to my nephews is the same exact message they've heard from their parents, but mine carries more weight. It is just different."

FROM STUMBLING TO STEALING

A teen is more likely to rationalize breaking a promise with a parent *who should be giving me these things anyway*, than they are with their aunt or uncle.

One father of a young teen who had just signed a *Just Say No* Promise Agreement with her uncle, told her, "You know, if you break this agreement, and continue to take those rewards, that would be the same thing as stealing from him."

BRINGING IN THE HEAVY HITTERS … THE GRANDPARENTS!

Grandma, Grandpa, Lita, Papa, Gammy, NaNa, and Poppy are just some of the names grandparents take these days. In Ireland you might be called Daddo or Seanmhair, in Italy Nonno, in Greece YaYa, in Africa Babu, and in Croatia Baka. In China you might be referred to as YeYe or Wai Gong depending on if you are the paternal or maternal grandfather; same goes in Sweden where you might be FarMor or MorMor. In Hawaii you might actually go by the regal sounding name of TuTu Kane.

Regardless of what name your grandson or granddaughter has for you, the respect and influence you have with them is considerable. Among other things, you represent to them a long life and wisdom. If you make a pact with them, it is likely that they will adhere to it on the basis of your strong relationship.

You can make a tremendous impact on the life of a teen. Be a great guide to the grandchild, niece, or nephew in your life!

CHAPTER 5

THE *JUST SAY NO* PROMISE AGREEMENT

There are two different Promise Agreements in the back of this book.

1. WITHOUT REWARDS:

This one does not include any added rewards to your teen for saying no. This agreement might be chosen for a variety of reasons:

1. The teen might come from a household where the rewards in question are already being provided to the student. In this case, the teen sees it as a way of *earning* those rewards. It is a gesture of them carrying their share of the responsibility that is expected from their family.
2. The teen might want to make the commitment without burdening any of their family members with the financial cost of paying for rewards.
3. The parents might believe that, for their teen, it is better that they commit to saying no without being provided added incentives.

4. Some teens who sign the Promise Agreement consider it to be a pledge to themselves to do those things that are considered to be difficult or hard, in an effort to create a better future for themselves.

Despite not having rewards attached, this agreement is still a pledge of honor. It is still a very powerful agreement. It still gives them a great excuse for their peers. It still leads them to a big life.

However, for it to succeed, it is *essential* that this agreement be as strictly adhered to, and as fully enforced, as the agreement that offers rewards. *Just saying no* cannot be viewed as *optional*, just because there are no rewards. As stated in both books, the myriad of benefits from *just saying no* is reward enough!

2. WITH REWARDS:

The other Promise Agreement in the back of this book spells out added rewards and incentives that the guides offer their teen in return for their promise to say no (entirely) to any sort of drugs, alcohol, or tobacco during their high school years. It creates a contract between the teenager and the most important, loving, and caring people he or she has in their life.

PREPARING FOR THE SIGNING

Below are a few things you will want to do before you meet with your teen to sign the fill-in-the-blank *Just Say No* Promise Agreement at the end of this book:

- Read both parts of this book. Have your teen read the book *Just Say No* (or the second half of this book).

- Determine before the meeting what added incentives you will offer your teen.
- Quantify the cost and sacrifice that you will incur by giving these incentives.
- Quantify the after-tax benefits your teen derives from *Just Saying No*. Explain how many hours per week they would have to work to replicate those benefits.
- Ask them if they have any reservations about signing the agreement. Have them acknowledge that they are voluntarily agreeing to the terms on their own volition and are not under any sort of duress or coercion.
- Make clear what both parties expect from each other.
- Explain your motivation. Discuss not only your loving desire that they create a great foundation for a successful life, but also talk about your self-interest of being able to relax at night, knowing they are a trustworthy, sober driver who is avoiding the perils of binge-drinking, drug-use, and smoking. Explain how important it is to you that they set a good example for their siblings to follow.
- Ask if there are any other questions or concerns that need to be addressed.
- Make copies for everyone; including their parents, if you are not the parent. (You can download blank Promise Agreements at www.justsayno.org.)

You are about to create a powerful and tangible tool for your teen to confront a storm that threatens their health, well-being, and future! Congrats!

CHAPTER 6

STANDING UP TO BEER PRESSURE

Recently, I attended a local symposium hosted by a group of middle school teachers. One teacher asked the audience of parents if any of them put restrictions on how their child can use their cell phone. After listening to a variety of approaches parents took, the teacher said, "The reason I ask this is because half of my 8th grade students say that they sleep with their phone."

It was a sobering statement for many of the parents. The teacher then added, "Whenever there is a problem amongst the kids, regarding bullying, hurt feelings, or misunderstandings that begin with gossip, I will ask the kids, 'When exactly, did all of this get started?' Inevitably, you will find out that it all started between midnight and 3 o'clock in the morning."

She suggested that one of the best things parents can do is have an open-monitoring policy where the student knows that at any time, without warning, they might have to hand the phone over to you, so that you can go through their activity on the phone. The teacher went on to say, "Your kids won't tell you this, but a lot of them *like having the excuse* that you monitor their phone. It comes in handy for them when one of their peers asks them to post a comment they really don't want to make, or download a photo they really don't want to have on their phone."

This same principle applies to standing up to the peer pressure to drink (*beer* pressure) and use drugs.

You might think that teens shouldn't have to rely on an excuse; that they should have the strength of character to say no whenever they want to, without having to justify themselves. But, think about it. When the most popular girl or guy in the school befriends your teen and wants to share a few drinks or smoke pot with him or her, do you really want them to have a back-and-forth conversation about whether or not your teen should partake?

One of the most tangible tools you can give your teen to confront *beer* pressure, is a great excuse!

CHAPTER 7

YOU DON'T EXPECT THIS TO ACTUALLY WORK, DO YOU?

One evening I was presenting the *Just Say No* plan to a group of parents. Toward the end of my talk, one of the parents asked, "What happens if your kid breaks the agreement?"

I replied, "Oh, you don't expect this thing to actually *work* do you?"

We all laughed, because we all recognize the very real possibility (some would say the *probability*) that our son or daughter will not honor the Promise Agreement.

This actually highlights one of the best features of the *Just Say No* plan.

THE PERFECT AGREEMENT FOR A 'STUMBLE'

Soon after our son got his driver's license, we presented a *Just Say No* Promise Agreement that spelled out the conditions he would have to follow in return for use of a gassed up, insured car (and other incentives). As you can imagine, we spent a lot of time (an hour or two) discussing the agreement with him:

- We were not making this offer lightly.
- He was under no obligation to sign the agreement. It was entirely his choice.
- Now was the time to point out any conditions he considered unreasonable.
- Frankly, it was expensive for us to provide him these added incentives.
- We were empowering him because he was using good judgment.
- We quantified the incentives which were equivalent to him working all day Saturday and two weekday evenings.
- We suggested that he consider it *his job* to *Just Say No*. A well-paying job!
- In return, we would sleep better at night, knowing that he was acting responsibly, driving sober, and being smart. Better sleep was a good thing, since we'd have to wake up early to go to work to pay for all of this!
- If he broke any of the conditions of the Promise Agreement, the incentives would end immediately.

We also included in the agreement that he adhere to the laws of the city, which included an 11:00 pm curfew for anyone under 18 years of age. "You can be early, and that's fine. You can even be late. How can we stop you? We're not going to chase you down. But, if you are late, we take the keys." **(I now recommend that you do not include a time curfew in the agreement for fear that a teen might drive too fast to get home on time, which is never good.)**

He eagerly signed the agreement. I am sure that he suspected at the time, as did we, that he was probably getting the better end of the bargain.

Then, he was off! It was the 4th of July, and he had plans to meet some of his friends at the park to watch fireworks!

"See ya!"

STUMBLE ON DAY ONE!

When he finally got home at 11:30, I was surprised that he was 30 minutes late. He was surprised that I was still awake. Both of us were surprised that the other one was surprised!

I said, "If this wasn't so ridiculous, I'd be really upset right now."

"Whattyamean?"

"Really? The very first night, and you're a half-hour late?" I asked.

"I had to take Justin home,"

"Okay. But, I need the keys."

"What!? Did you want me to just abandon Justin, and not take him home?"

I said, "No, you make your own choices. But, we have an agreement."

He was as furious as I would have been as a 16-year old, if I had been asked to return the car keys. He threw them on the table and charged upstairs to his room.

And that was all.

There was no yelling. No long arguments about what the punishment would be. The consequences were already *literally spelled out* in the agreement all of us had signed.

There was no need for a tense debate back and forth regarding ramifications that had already been clearly agreed upon. We didn't experience the stress that comes from arguing over what a reasonable punishment should be, or how long it would last.

That is the day I became 100% convinced that the *Just Say No* Promise Agreement was one of the best tools in the world for helping young teenagers transition into responsible adults.

A few days later, when he asked when he was getting use of the car again, my reaction was *basically never*. He had caused our agreement to be terminated. It was null and void.

"If you want to enter into another agreement, we're open to the idea, but it is up to you. You have to figure out a way to rebuild some trust here."

My wife and I were not in any hurry. The loss of the wheels had made it even more apparent to everyone that he had indeed received the better part of the bargain.

To his great credit, he did exactly that. He signed a new agreement and from that point forward he always honored the terms of the contract.

DID HE ACTUALLY ABIDE BY ALL OF THE TERMS OF THE AGREEMENT?

Can I be certain that our son didn't sneak a beer or a smoke here or there? No, there is no way to know for sure. A friend of mine once asked, "Now that he's all grown up and out of college, why don't you just ask him?"

My answer might sound about as strange to you as it did to my friend, but the truth is I don't really care. Sure, one of our hopes was to have him adhere 100% to his end of the bargain. And, I have no reason to doubt that he did. But we never lost sight of the *main goal* we had, and that was to *just get him through* those four dangerous years of high school, unscathed by drugs, alcohol, and tobacco. We are incredibly grateful that we were able to do that. Did he sneak a beer or two, here and there? Don't know. Don't care.

However, it isn't the easiest thing in the world to get the smell of smoke out of clothes, alcohol off the breath, or ashes out of the car. And, although teens are very clever, intoxication of any kind cannot always be so easily masked.

ANOTHER ARROW IN YOUR ARSENAL

If the best you can do is dramatically curtail bad behavior, then by all means, do the best you can do! If they cheat, but pass on that 2nd, 3rd, and 4th beer, keep fighting for every inch of higher ground you can gain. If your teen avoids the group of daily pot smokers, but bums a cigar once in a while, just keep working your plan. Savor the small victories, and keep the big goal in mind.

Consider high school an ongoing battle. Fire every available arrow you have at the threat. Consider the *Just Say No* Promise Agreement as a great arrow in your arsenal.

CHAPTER 8

10 QUESTIONS ABOUT THE *JUST SAY NO* PLAN

One day I was talking to a good friend of mine who had just read my book *Seeing Past Friday Night*. He had a son who was a junior in high school. He said,

"Garry, I like your book, but I kind of have a problem with the message of more-or-less *bribing* my kid with rewards for doing things he should already be doing anyway."

I replied, "You *do* know that your son drives a nicer car than I do, right? Is it really that egregious to require some responsible behavior in return?"

A lot of kids today are provided car privileges with insurance and a full tank of gas. Others receive allowances, money for clothes, or dollars necessary to participate in sports or other extracurricular activities. When is the last time you saw a kid without a smartphone? Did *you* have one of those growing up? Parents are *already* paying for some of those *added* rewards.

"Isn't it unrealistic to think that our teens can *just say no* 100% of the time? Isn't it inevitable that they are going to 'experiment'?"

Actually, no. Recent studies show that more than half of all high school students have never tried marijuana or taken a single puff of a cigarette. That means that millions of high school kids *are* saying no, *all* day long, *every* day. If you think about it, is it really all that difficult of a thing to do? Up until now, they have done it all of their lives, 100% of the time.

But, even if you believe that it is inevitable, the *Just Say No* Promise Agreement shines brightest when there *has been a stumble*, because a benchmark has been set. You have a signed document that literally spells out the consequences in advance! From there, you can get back on track.

What is more realistic? Believing that your teen can *Just Say No* during high school, or believing that they can successfully 'experiment' with drugs, alcohol, and tobacco without negative consequences?

It is very difficult for a teen to elevate above the expectations of their parents. So, expect them to be a hero!

"I would be absolutely shocked if *my* kid got into a problem with that stuff."

You certainly know your son or daughter better than anyone, so you're probably right. But, you might be cautioned by the narcotics officer who describes the absolute shock that parents have when he explains that their child has been arrested on drug charges.

"I don't like that the plan is so *materialistic*."

This is a valid concern for many parents. However, for better or worse, *we* live in a materialistic world. Even as adults, we are often motivated by financial rewards. Sometimes we *self*-motivate ourselves with the incentive of a nice dinner out, or a 3-day vacation for completing a project. As long as the rewards encourage us to achieve *worthy* goals, they can inspire us to do great things. But, you can avoid materialism altogether by choosing the Promise Agreement that does not include rewards.

"We simply cannot afford this financially."

Understood! If you are feeling the extraordinary financial pressure of raising a family, like we did, you might consider these alternatives.

- **Identify 'rewards' you already provide** (tuition, allowance, phone).
- **Enlist the troops!** Invite the grandparents, aunts, and uncles to join in and sign an agreement with your son or daughter. They will often welcome the opportunity to help.
- **Appeal to their highest character.** Explain the dilemma you face; that your funds are limited, but that you want them to sign the Promise Agreement without rewards. You want this for their well-being, for your peace of mind, and for the example that it will set for their siblings. You want them to be a hero.

"We did our share of stuff when we were kids, and *we all survived*."

Actually, if we are honest with ourselves, we didn't all survive. Few of us can say that we do not have a friend, classmate, or family member who was not seriously injured from the ravages of addiction, car accidents, or health problems that directly resulted from drugs, alcohol, or tobacco.

But, putting that aside for a minute, below are three more reasons why today's world is a whole new ballgame:

1. Pot was illegal when we were in high school; now, states are making it legal.
2. Prescription drugs are at an all-time high in America.
3. New inventive ways of getting high that never even occurred to us; ways that don't even involve drugs or alcohol, are commonplace today.

"I'm concerned that if my kids don't become accustomed to drinking responsibly now, they will go crazy after they graduate."

My own parents had this same concern. So, in our agreement, my siblings and I were allowed to drink an occasional glass of wine or beer at dinner at home, when they were there. This gave us a familiarity, while ensuring that we did not drive, or engage in high-risk activities, while consuming alcohol.

But, let's not forget that a teenager's brain is still developing throughout high school. Hopefully, they will be better equipped, after high school, to make better decisions. They will also have the added maturity that naturally comes from observing the world around them during their teen years.

"We act as if these kids are 'broken'; like they're bad kids that have to be 'fixed' or something. I am around these kids all the time, and I can tell you that they're good kids."

This comment was made at a community leader roundtable, convened to discuss the growing drug and alcohol problem occurring in the local high schools.

My first thought was, of course this isn't *our kid's* fault. They're 13-14-15 years old! *They* didn't have anything to do with creating this drug-saturated environment. It is the responsible of our societal leaders and the adult generation to create a safe culture and a safe environment for our children.

In reality, however, it is counterproductive to allocate blame. Concentrating on forces and institutions beyond our control only serves to give us a false sense of security that we can assign our teen's war against drug use and binge drinking to other people. We must be honest with ourselves and realize that the one thing that always keeps our teens safe is within *their* own control. *Just Saying No*.

When we tell our kids to *Just Say No*, we are not suggesting they are *broken*. Instead, we are saying that *they are in control of their lives*. That they are *powerful*.

Just Saying No says yes to a powerful future.

"This might be good for our *middle* child, but we don't need this for our *oldest*."

Do it anyway—for these reasons:

- It familiarizes your oldest teen with a written contract.
- It gives him or her a great excuse to help fend off incredible peer pressure.
- Most importantly, the oldest child sets an important precedent for the younger siblings to follow. *If my sister and brother could do it for me, I should follow through and set a similar example for my younger brother.*

"Can't they just figure this out *along the way*?

Three to four years ago, your young teen was 10 years old! They have never seen a single friend of theirs go homeless, lose a job, develop heart disease from smoking; or drop out of college as a result of drugs or alcohol. You and I have seen those things. They haven't!

How can we expect them to share our perspectives on the dangers of opioids? They don't even know what opioids are! You and I have learned lessons from making some good decisions and some bad ones. Why not pass those lessons onto our kids?

If our teenagers refuse to study history by asking their elders (that would be us) for advice, then they relegate themselves to living their life as a continual experiment. A guide is often defined as a person who shows the way to someone who hasn't been there before. That's why *you* are the guide!

CHAPTER 9

WHAT IS THE MOST DANGEROUS SUBSTANCE FOR YOUR TEEN?

Of all the bad stuff out there, what is the most dangerous one for our kids? Included in the list below, is the scariest, most sinister, most dangerous substance of all:

- Barbiturates
- Angel Dust
- Cocaine
- Alcohol
- Heroin
- Mushrooms
- Oxycodone
- Hallucinogens
- "Molly"
- Cigarettes
- Bath Salts
- Sniffed Glue
- Chewing Tobacco
- Opioids
- Morphine
- LSD

- Cough Syrup
- Spice Herbs
- Snuff
- Methamphetamines
- Inhalants
- Diet Pills
- Anabolic Steroids
- Depressants
- Marijuana

The *worst* of these is whichever one your child ends up having a problem with.

You don't need to know an upper from a downer, or a stimulant from a depressant. And neither does your teen. None of that matters.

IT DOESN'T NEED TO BE COMPLICATED!

Some people think that we have to explore the nuances of every substance and the effects that each one has on the human body. Not really. You'd have to be a pharmacist to figure it all out, and it just doesn't matter anyway. What purpose would it serve?

We often think the world has become too complicated for simple answers. The truth is, there might not be easy answers, but there are *simple* ones. Our kids just have to have the courage to do what they know is right.

Just Say No is not necessarily *easy* (although, in high school, I never found it to be particularly difficult). But, it is unquestionably *simple*.

So, forget about reading up on all the different substances that can be abused. Keep it simple and *Just Say No* to *all* of them.

CHAPTER 10

THE POWER OF *JUST SAYING NO*

In the book that your teen will read, there is a chapter titled *"The Power of Saying No."* When you read it, keep in mind that there are ancillary benefits they derive from the mere act of signing a contract and standing out from the crowd.

It teaches them:

A CONTRACT, A COVENANT, A PROMISSORY NOTE.

The *Just Say No* Promise Agreement is a simple agreement with a handful of terms and conditions. But, from the perspective of your teenage daughter or son, it goes to the heart of how much freedom, liberty, and power they have in their life right now. It also spells out the boundaries and responsibilities they have to live up to.

For many, it will be the first contract they ever sign.

Better to have them learn about contracts, by having one with *you* first, than by being surprised in their early 20s by having their car repossessed. If done correctly, this is an opportunity to teach your teen about negotiation, committing to a plan, and pledging their honor with a signature.

THE PROMISE AGREEMENT ALSO TEACHES THEM:

- They can stand apart from the crowd and the world doesn't end!
- *Just Saying No* will often reveal their *true* friends.
- They can gain extraordinary freedoms and opportunities if they are willing to self-impose rational boundaries in their life.
- Keeping true to the contract creates *a quiet confidence* from knowing that they can actually control their life.

Keeping their promise builds character, creates trust, and strengthens their relationships with their guides, their friends, and their siblings!

CHAPTER 11

UH OH ...
WE DIDN'T THINK OF EVERYTHING

My wife and I know firsthand that some of the best Promise Agreements are made between an uncle and aunt, and their niece or nephew. But they sometimes come with a surprise or two.

THE SURPRISE PHONE CALL:

One day, I received a phone call from our niece.

She said, "Hi, Uncle Garry. Hey, you know that agreement we have going on with the no drinking and everything?"

"I sure do."

"Well, it has worked out really great. But, with these last three months of senior year approaching, I think I'd like to go ahead and cancel the agreement. Now, I know that sounds bad, but it's not like I'm going to go out and start drinking like crazy, or anything like that. But, we have these play parties coming up, and then graduation, where I will probably have a beer or two, and I didn't want to keep using the gas card and stuff you guys are giving me."

My first thought was one of respect for my niece for being honest and upfront with me and my wife regarding her intentions. My second thought went to the idea of her drinking at the various graduation parties that, of course, would likely result in her driving from one party to the other. Although it had been part of the agreement that either party could terminate it at any time, we hadn't anticipated that she might do that at such a strategically poor time.

I scrambled. My first response was to point out to her that, if in fact she was only talking about having a beer or two at each party, and if there were only 15 parties between now and graduation, then she was giving up about $20 per beer.

"Those are pretty expensive beers," I said.

"I know it is. But, still, I think it is something that I want to do."

So, we made one last-ditch effort. "Okay. It's your decision. But, before you decide this for sure, we are going to make you one more offer. If you extend our agreement through the end of July, we will throw in an additional bonus of two hundred dollars."

There were a few seconds of silence on the other end of the phone, before I heard her say, "Ugh. Can I think about that for a little bit?"

I said, "Sure. But keep in mind that you will probably not look back at this summer and wish you had drunk a dozen beers at the parties. But you might look back and wish you had that extra money to spend."

The next day she accepted our offer.

A year later, at the family Thanksgiving dinner, I asked my niece if she thought that our agreement had made any impact on her.

She said, "Not a whole lot. I don't think that I would have been drinking much anyway. But it did sort of affect who I hung around with quite a bit."

"How's that?" I asked.

"Well, I found out real quick that when my friends left a party to go off and drink until midnight, it wasn't much fun sitting around watching them get all silly. So, following them around didn't last too long."

Somehow, her answer didn't disappoint my wife and me. Could you really say that we *bribed* our niece; that we overly enticed her with dollars, when dollars for her were in short supply? Don't know. Don't care. She got through safely, which was our goal. Today, she still believes it was a great deal for her. We do too.

CHAPTER 12

11 More Things You Can Do to Keep Your Teen Safe

1. Limit their access to prescription drugs. If they are yours or their sibling's, lock them up! If unused or outdated, throw them out!

2. **Work closely with their doctor to minimize the prescription pain relievers**, whenever your son or daughter:
   - Suffers a sports injury,
   - Has their wisdom teeth removed, or
   - Has a surgery of any kind.

   Keep a close eye on them during this critical time. Know that illicit drug suppliers are specifically targeting your teen and will approach them to *replace* their pain medication.

3. **Limit alcohol visibility in your home**; an easy thing to do.

4. **Lead by example.** Drink responsibly. Remember that your teen is getting cues from you when you throw a party at your home with *your* friends.

5. **Identify crucial times of susceptibility and create alternative events they will enjoy, to compete with these critical times.** You know they are coming. You know *when* they are coming. Plan for it!
   - Spring Break
   - Play Parties
   - Prom
   - After-Game Parties
   - Sleepovers
   - Graduation Parties

6. **Prepare them for inevitable times of disappointment**; the breakup of a close friendship, being cut from the lacrosse team, a poor report card, losing the big part in the play, or not being invited to a party. When this happens, you probably cannot 'fix it'. But, you can help them implement The Four A's:
   a. **Anticipate** that big disappointments *will* occur from time to time, so that they are not blind-sided when they occur.
   b. **Assess the disappointment**, and keep it in its proper perspective.
   c. **Avoid knee-jerk reactions** where, in a fit of anger or sadness, they turn to drugs or alcohol thinking that it will be a quick fix.
   d. **Appreciate** what they have. You can sit down with them and list on paper those things for which they are super-grateful. Encourage them to direct their attention to the *good* things going on in their life.

7. **Anticipate times of great euphoria** (winning the basketball championship, a new friendship, being asked to a fun party, getting into the school of their choice). The Four A's will help with this too.

8. **Continually praise them for *saying no*.** When you are about to yell at your teen for not cutting the grass, maybe say instead, "You know, if that grass gets any higher, we're not going to be able to see the neighbor's house. But I want you to know that we really respect you for staying true to the agreement we signed. Now, go get that grass."

9. **Add a couple milestone rewards.** Along with the incentives you are giving, maybe you throw in milestone rewards along the way, such as shopping or dinner gift cards that they can share with their friends.

10. **Have extended family members reinforce the effort:** Having their aunt or uncle or grandparent meet with them periodically to reinforce the importance of staying strong goes a long way towards success.

11. **And for those who want to go the added distance … join them!** A strong statement you can make about how important it is for them to *Just Say No*, is to agree to do the same, throughout the length of the agreement. Too tough you say? If it's too tough for you, why would it be any easier for them? You're asking them to set an example. You can too!

CHAPTER 13

TYPES OF INCENTIVES AND REWARDS

A friend of mine, and his wife, offered their oldest son $500 upon graduation if he agreed to *Just Say No*. When he succeeded, they gathered up his younger brothers and sisters around the kitchen table, where they had spread out 500 one-dollar bills.

"Scan, you'd be surprised at how much money that looks like when it is spread out that way," he said.

I replied, "It *is* a lot of money. And they are after-tax dollars!"

He said, "You should have seen my younger kids. Their eyes were this big! They all said, 'I want to do it, I want to do it.' "

Do not underestimate the impact your teen's success will have on the others. They're watching!

HOW MUCH SHOULD YOU SPEND FOR INCENTIVES?

This is very difficult to decide. You have to consider so many factors.

- How much can we afford?

- At what point does this become too materialistic for our teen?
- What is *really* going to get our teen's attention?

THE LEAST EXPENSIVE APPROACH:

Least expensive are those things that you already provide them. Those might include:

- High School tuition
- Cell phones
- Cell phone and texting charges
- Use of a car
- Car insurance
- A gas card
- Athletic equipment
- Musical instruments
- Guitar lessons, karate classes, voice or dance lessons
- Summer sports camp
- Fees required for extracurricular activities

REMEMBER TO ENLIST HELP!

You might be surprised to find that extended family members are eager to throw in on the deal. A $20 monthly gift card to Starbucks might go a long way towards encouraging your teen to stay vigilant. It isn't always the amount involved, but just having the teen know that people who love them are going the extra mile to help them prepare for a big life.

THE 3 KINDS OF INCENTIVES:

Ongoing: Examples are limited use of a car, a gas card, or phone charges.

Milestone: Strategically timed rewards along the way, such as tickets to a college football game, a new pair of athletic shoes, weekend travel trips.

End Game: A reward given upon fulfillment of the Promise Agreement.

GET CREATIVE.

Tailor your rewards and incentives to the personal interests of your teen. Think what would be most exciting to them.

The Actress: A 3-day weekend trip to Times Square with tickets to a couple of Broadway plays and nice restaurants.

The Fly Fisherman: A weeklong trip to Jackson Hole, Wyoming where they can fish, kayak, and hike the wilderness.

The Horse Lover: A horseback riding trip to Flagstaff Arizona, where they can ride horses in the morning and ski in the afternoon.

The Reader: Arrange a meet and greet with their favorite author.

The 'Cash is King' Teen: For the teen who is more into instant gratification. Maybe this person is paid a monthly allowance of a predetermined amount.

The Golfer: Pebble Beach is open to the public with many packages to choose from! Or a golf trip to Ireland! Would he or she like to play Pinehurst?

The Adventurer: A train trip across America, from Chicago to Spokane in a Superliner Roomette!

The Biker: How about a new, tricked-out mountain bike?

Hard-To-Get-Tickets: Can you score tickets to see *Saturday Night Live*, the Super Bowl, or backstage passes to *Hamilton*.

How about that trip to Italy you always wanted to go on anyway? Get creative and have fun with it.

ENGAGE THE ENTIRE FAMILY

The *best* incentive is to create a win-win reward that you and the rest of the family can enjoy. That would *really* reveal your teen as a hero!

Some of this sounds expensive, because, well, some of it is. But weigh the cost against how much you might end up saving from the cost of car accidents, legal fees, medical bills, and lost scholarship dollars.

And remember, you always have the option of using the Promise Agreement that offers no add rewards.

Take the Promise Agreement and personalize it for your teen! (You can tear out the Agreements at the back of this book and make copies or download blank Promise Agreements at www.justsayno.org.)

AFTERWORD FOR PARENTS, GRANDPARENTS, AUNTS, AND UNCLES

Thank you for taking the time to read this book.

You are the line in the sand, the protector of the teen in your life. You are to be applauded for your efforts. It isn't a task for the faint of heart.

Hopefully, you picked up several good ideas in this book and will take this plan and make it your own. Tailor the plan to work best for your son, daughter, granddaughter, niece, or nephew.

I'd be very grateful for any thoughts or ideas you discover along the way that might help us improve the tools and concepts we use at JustSayNo.org to help young adults. We are all in this together!

We root for you to help your teen achieve heroic dreams!

Because, every story needs a hero. Every hero needs a guide!

Garrett K. Scanlon
www.JustSayNo.org

How to Bring JustSayNo.org to Your School, Parent Group, Church, Rotary, SADD/MADD Functions, Web Tribe, Red Ribbon Week, or Prevention Event!

Garrett Scanlon is available to speak at your school or organization and bring copies of this book, *Just Say No for Parents, Grandparents, Aunts, and Uncles*. Each presentation is tailored specifically to your group or event.

If you would like to:

- Schedule Garrett to speak,
- Obtain bulk-rate copies of *Just Say No,*
- Subscribe free to our blog,
- Get involved with the *Just Say No* Program,
- Sponsor a school,
- Refer us to groups,
- Download a free Promise Agreement,
- Donate added rewards to encourage teens to *Just Say No*,
- Provide us with added ideas to improve our message, or
- Tell us *your* story …

Please visit: www.JustSayNo.org

PART TWO

Just Say No

Because Every Story Needs a Hero

Includes a *Promise Agreement* to Earn
Added Rewards for Saying No to
Binge Drinking, Drug Use, and Smoking
in High School

GARRETT K. SCANLON

Author of *Seeing Past Friday Night*

JustSayNo.org

BALLYLONGFORD BOOKS

Copyright © 2017 by Garrett K. Scanlon

JustSayNo.org
250 Civic Center Dr. 5th Floor CASTO
Columbus, OH 43215

All rights reserved. No part of this book may be reproduced in any manner or form whatsoever, by any means, electronically or mechanically, including photocopying or recording, or by any information or retrieval system, or in relation to goods and/or seminars (including seminars, workshops, training programs, classes, etc.) without the expressed, written permission from the publisher, except by reviewer, who may quote brief passages for reviews or articles about the book.

Disclaimer: The author of this publication is not an attorney and the reader should not consider the information contained herein to be legal advice. The draftsman of the Just Say No Promise Agreement at the end of this book is not an attorney and this agreement is not, and is not intended to be, a legally enforceable contract, but merely an aid for young adults and their sponsors. Reader shall hold Garrett Scanlon harmless from any and all claims, lawsuits, demands, causes of action, liability, loss, damage and/or injury, of any kind. If the reader wants to create an enforceable contract, he or she should consult an attorney.

Scanlon, Garrett K.

    Just Say No—Because Every Story Needs a Hero–Includes a Promise Agreement to Earn Added Rewards for Saying No to Binge Drinking, Drug Use, and Smoking in High School/
    Garrett K. Scanlon–Columbus, Ohio

ISBN: 978-0-9961943-2-7 (Softcover)
ISBN: 978-0-9961943-4-1 (eBook)
Library of Congress Control Number: 2017943395

Summary: A powerful plan for teens to receive added incentives and rewards to *Just Say No* to drugs, alcohol, and tobacco during their high school years; and to dream heroic dreams and prepare for a big future. Includes a *Just Say No* Promise Agreement that can be signed by teens and their parents, grandparents, aunts, and uncles. Because, every story needs a hero.

Printed and bound in the United States of America.
First printing 2017. Excerpts are available for reprinting in your publication.

Author is available to speak at your elementary school, middle school, high school, parent group, Rotary, PSR group, church group, and drug and alcohol prevention events.

Visit www.JustSayNo.org

Cover image courtesy of iStockphoto.com
Front cover design: Kristine Coplin
Text design: by www.tothepointsolutions.com

This book is dedicated to that one person ...

Who is not afraid to take on a challenge;

Who has the courage to add some discipline to his or her life;

Who understands that life can be tough, but becomes infinitely easier when we are tough on ourselves;

That one person who dreams heroic dreams;

Who is willing to make a promise, keep it, and upon a job well done, look the other person in the eye, shake hands, and say thank you!

This book is dedicated to that one person—You!

CONTENTS

	A Letter to You	77
1.	Every Story Needs a Hero	81
2.	You Have the Right to Dream Heroic Dreams	85
3.	A Collision Course	89
4.	How I Got the Use of a Car	91
5.	Seeing Past Friday Night	93
6.	And He's My Friend!	95
7.	The Power of Saying No	97
8.	The Great Paradox	99
9.	Incentives and Rewards: The *Just Say No* Promise Agreement	103
10.	Free Samples and Other Sales Tactics	107
11.	How to Prepare for Your Polygraph	111
12.	"What in the World Does Someone Like Me Have to Look Forward To?"	113
13.	Finding Your Guitar	117
14.	The Two Imposters—Triumph and Disaster	121
15.	"I Wish I Had Smoked More Cigarettes."	125
16.	A Letter to Your Future Self	127
	Thank You!	129
	About the Author	131
	How to Bring *Just Say No* to Your Group	132
	Just Say No Agreement with Rewards	133
	Just Say No Agreement—No Rewards	135

A LETTER TO YOU

At *JustSayNo*.org, we believe:
- **You are in control,**
- **You are powerful,**
- **You are a hero in the making.**

Up until now, you've had the same friends for many years. You knew all of their parents, the coaches, and the teachers. You were surrounded by a village of great people preparing you for your next journey—high school.

Now it's up to you. The transition from a middle school student to a young, strong, responsible adult has begun. And the stakes are high.

HIGH SCHOOL

Along with an entirely new set of teachers, coaches, and friends, you will be granted a variety of new freedoms. You will learn how to drive a car, possibly get a part-time job, and participate in new activities.

Instead of a village of supporters making your every decision, it will be up to you to make some of the most important decisions of your life. The choices you make now will have enormous consequences for you, well into your future. And like every other young adult your age, all of this comes at a time when you have a relatively low level of experience. Your most *critical* decision will be how well you confront drugs, alcohol, and tobacco during your high school years.

A FALSE SENSE OF SECURITY

In today's world, it is a false sense of security to believe that *society-at-large* will keep you safe from ingesting drugs, alcohol, or tobacco in high school. You cannot rely on strict laws to keep you safe. Because, let's be honest, you can always break the law. You can't delegate the war on drugs to homeland security or law enforcement, because, the bottom line is this:

On Friday night, when you find out that you …

- Were cut from the basketball team,
- Failed that chemistry exam your parents said you better ace,
- Did not get the part in the play you so desperately wanted, or
- Got a text that your girlfriend or boyfriend wants to break up,

And the person next to you says, "Who cares? Let's go get high."

When this happens, the police will not be there. Your teachers will not be there. Your coaches will not be there. Drug counselors will not be there. Even your parents will not be there.

THE GOOD NEWS IS …

No matter *where* you are,

No matter *what time* of day or night it is,

No matter *how often* the critical decisions have to be made,

There is one person who will always be there …

You.

Wherever you go, *you* will always be there! This is a good thing, because *you* are the one person who can *Just Say No*, **every single time**.

It can feel kind of daunting; that it's all up to you. But, isn't it also kind of liberating? It empowers you. Rather than being dependent on a dozen unknown forces out there, *you* can be the hero that keeps you safe. The hero that keeps your brother or sister safe!

Frankly, at *JustSayNo*.org, we believe the war on drugs, binge-drinking, and smoking does not *end* with you. It *begins* with you. It is a confrontation ...

You can win.

You must win.

You will win.

This book is designed to be read in about 30 minutes. It is short, simple, and extremely powerful. It includes a proven plan of action that has worked for thousands of people, along with a *Just Say No* Promise Agreement (in the back of this book) that you will sign with a parent, grandparent, aunt, or uncle that creates added incentives and rewards for you to confront the storm of drugs, alcohol, and tobacco.

No matter your limitations or challenges, you were designed for greatness. You will be somebody's hero. You might not yet be aware of the superpowers you possess, but you will soon discover that they are perfectly suited for a big future.

Read the book, find a guide, and prepare for the storm.

Because every story needs a hero.

Garrett K. Scanlon

www.JustSayNo.org

CHAPTER 1

Every Story Needs a Hero

Any novelist, screenwriter, or playwright will tell you that every story needs **a hero**. The hero is on **a journey**. Then, **a crisis** occurs; an enormous threat or challenge that the hero must defeat or overcome.

Out of a cast of characters, emerges **a guide**; an ally that comes alongside to help the hero. There are always **high stakes** involved. There is a **plan of action** resulting in a **resolute outcome**.

For a story to resonate with us, it must always have these elements. Because, well, that's life!

- **A Hero**
- **A Journey**
- **A Crisis or Threat**
- **A Guide**
- **High Stakes**
- **A Plan of Action**
- **A Resolute Outcome**

In this true-life story, *you* are the hero. You might not *think* you're a hero, because heroes do not always *feel* particularly heroic during their high school years. You haven't even identified all of your super-powers yet! But, you *do* have them. The problem is, those powers don't always apply to what is important to you *right now*.

Some of your greatest skills and abilities that will help you become a great novelist, or entrepreneur, or firefighter, or nurse, or teacher, or Army Ranger, or songwriter are usually unrelated to scoring touchdowns or starring in the school play. You probably don't want anyone telling you, "Don't worry about that. Your day will come." But, what William Shakespeare wrote, is very true: *We know what we are, but not what we may be.*

The Hero: Regardless of any limitations or challenges you have, you are truly designed for greatness. It is your birthright to dream heroic dreams.

The Journey: You are on a *crucial* journey in high school, with a cast of characters that includes new friends, new teachers, and new coaches. You have to juggle a changing physiology, peer pressure, and the emotional swings that occur when you ace a big test one day and get cut from the soccer team the next.

The Crisis/Threat: A storm is coming. A storm that can leave behind a path of incredible destruction. The single biggest threat to you living a powerful life is you making bad decisions regarding the use of drugs, alcohol, and tobacco.

The Guides: Your parents, grandparents, aunts, and uncles are your guides! If you are Rocky Balboa, then they are your trusted fight-trainer, Mickey, who prepared him to survive all 15 rounds. Think about it. They are the ones who are truly in your corner, rooting for you to triumph all 4 years!

The High Stakes: At stake is:
- A loss of respect,
- Team suspensions,

- Loss of friendships,
- DWI's/DUI's/OWI's,
- Attorney fees,
- Suffering grades,
- Loss of car privileges,
- Addiction, and
- A risk that your siblings will follow suit.

The Plan-of-Action: The *Just Say No* Promise Agreement spells out the terms and conditions required for you to defeat the threat and receive added rewards along the way. (You can tear out the Agreements at the back of this book and make copies or download blank Promise Agreements at www.justsayno.org.)

This Story's Resolute Outcome: Rewards begin immediately and victory comes at graduation when you, the hero, shake hands with your guides on a job well done. Like all heroes, you will fulfill the best version of yourself, and your greatest reward will be the strong example you give your siblings, and others, to follow.

The stakes are high. We root for the hero. We root for *you*!

Are you up for the challenge?

CHAPTER 2

YOU HAVE THE RIGHT TO DREAM HEROIC DREAMS

A lot of people think that it was a waste of time to write this book. They echo a lot of what you hear and read from so many self-proclaimed *experts*. Basically, the sentiment is that today's teens are too self-obsessed and screen-obsessed to have a serious discussion about anything important.

You hear things like:

Might as well wait until they're older. They're gonna do what they're gonna do. There's not a whole lot of thinking going on there.

Teenagers are incapable of taking anything seriously. You're talking to them about their future—to a group of people who think they're invincible. Good luck with that.

And, how many times have you heard this one?

Heck, their brains aren't even fully formed until they're 25 years old!

I usually point out that the last time I checked, their brains were fully enough formed to show us how to work the settings on our remote control devices.

Do you buy into those low expectations? I don't. I think the exact opposite is true.

Sure, it might take a bit of time to figure out all of the ground rules, and how you're going to fit into the scheme of things. But, there is nobody out there who wants a bigger life, a more heroic life for yourself, than you do.

In fact, I think that your generation is more fired up about the idea of having a positive impact on others, your family, and the world around you than any other generation in recent memory. And, if there are ideas out there that will help you reach these goals, you're open to listening.

We're told that it's naïve to think that you or your friends have the maturity and fortitude to *just say no* to drugs, alcohol, and tobacco all the time. But, study after study shows that millions of high school freshman, sophomores, juniors, and seniors do exactly that, all day long, every day. Millions! And, we're supposed to believe that you can't be one of those millions? Well, that's just plain stupid. Of course you can! In fact, statistically, the odds say that you *will* be one of those teens who *just say no*.

It is hard to imagine how great life will be for you. You have the good fortune of living in the freest, most prosperous nation, not only in the world, but in the *history* of the world. On top of that, there are tens of millions of baby boomers (born between 1946 and 1964) who will be retiring over the next 15 years, opening up for your generation an endless supply of fulfilling, prosperous career opportunities. And you only need one of them! As much as you enjoy being a teen, you're going to *love* your twenties.

BUT FIRST, THERE IS A STORM COMING.

You didn't create the storm, but it's up to you to weather it. And, if you have a brother or sister, you have to help them get through it too. Because the storm of binge drinking, smoking, and drug use in high school, brings with it the potential for devastating pain. *Physical*, *financial*, and *emotional* pain. It leaves in its path:

- Wrecked cars,
- Serious injury,
- Legal bills,
- Team expulsions,
- Unwanted addictions,
- Poor classroom performance,
- Broken friendships, and
- Harm to your siblings.

And it is headed your way.

THE BEST WAY TO CONFRONT THE THREAT IS TO *JUST SAY NO*.

Not, no *because of this*,

Not, no *because of that*,

No, *because you said so*!

Just Saying No empowers you. *Just Saying No* puts you in control.

The single biggest factor determining your ability to achieve your dreams is not:

- How much money you have,
- How smart you are,
- How attractive you are,
- How good of an athlete you are, or even
- How hard you work.

It is how well you confront the storm ahead of you. There are many rich, smart, nice, attractive, athletic, and hard-working people who have jeopardized their health, career, and family-life by the time they have graduated from high school; all because they didn't recognize that in high school they were on a collision course …

CHAPTER 3

A COLLISION COURSE

Do you consider yourself to be a good car driver, or someone who *will* be a good driver as soon as you get your license?

You will have taken all of the necessary driving tests, spent time on the road, and are probably a relatively conscientious person. You probably have what it takes to be a good driver. So far, so good?

NOW ASK YOURSELF THIS:

Will you be a better driver four years from now, after you've had 48 more months behind the wheel?

Regardless of age, everyone knows the answer to that question. The more time you spend driving in rain, ice, snow, hail, sleet, high winds, blinding sun, and thick fog, the better driver you become. Driving under different conditions, such as when you are stressed or tired, in mountainous regions, or on long trips; this makes you a better driver.

Because, that is how experience works!

ONE MORE QUESTION:

Do you consider yourself to be good at confronting

drugs, alcohol, and tobacco? You probably are mature for your age and use good judgment. So far, so good?

But, will you have an even better insight after 48 months of watching some of your friends get kicked off sports teams, wreck cars, be cited for DUI's, or injure others? Will you know more after seeing the carnage left behind from a drug overdose? From seeing their younger brothers and sisters follow bad examples?

Sure. Because, that is how experience works.

IT IS NOT A MATTER OF MATURITY!

Your four years of high school might end up being the riskiest and most dangerous four-year period of your life. Likely, you will never again have a time in your life when you are granted such an explosion of new freedoms and responsibilities while having such a relatively low level of experience.

Nobody is saying that you are immature. You are probably more mature than a lot of people who are twice your age.

But, it is not a matter of *maturity*!

It is a matter of *experience*!

DEFY THE VILLAINS.

The best advice you can give yourself is to stay strong for another day. The single act of confronting drugs, alcohol, and tobacco in high school puts you way ahead of the game.

In the meantime, there are real villains in this story who are counting on you making a lot of mistakes.

But, they will be disappointed.

Because, in this story, you are a hero.

CHAPTER 4

How I Got the Use of a Car

It was a sunny day in June, the summer before my freshman year in high school. I had just finished playing basketball with some of the kids in the neighborhood, and was chugging down some lemonade from the fridge when my dad said he had something to discuss with me.

My first thought was, *Uh oh, what'd I do now?* But, from his tone, it didn't sound like I was in any trouble.

"Garry, your mom and I would like to make you an offer."

Hmm, this was weird. I wondered, *what's up with this?*

"As you know, you're going to be starting high school soon, and with that comes a certain amount of added freedom. You are going to be making a lot of decisions when your mom and I are not around. We also recognize that there are going to be a lot of temptations thrown your way. Some of the ones we are most concerned about are drinking and smoking and drugs," he said.

Now I got it. I knew where this was headed. So, I stopped him. "Oh Dad, don't worry about that. I'm not..."

I was about to explain that I knew all about that stuff and that he didn't need to take time explaining it to me, blah, blah, blah. The last thing I wanted was one of those *awkward* talks.

But he interrupted me.

"I am sure you will use your common sense. But this isn't just about you. You see Garry, with all of the things your mom has done for you, and for your brothers and sisters, I can't stand the thought of her having to spend a single minute worrying at night that one of you might get in trouble with any of that stuff. So this is what I'm prepared to do."

The conversation had gone from awkward to serious.

Dad said, "If you agree to not drink, smoke, or try drugs of any kind, then we will make sure that you always have access to a car when you get your license. We will also pay towards the gas and car insurance. And, we'll throw in a reasonable monthly allowance."

I'm sure my dad noticed my eyebrows rise as I tilted my head forward.

I was confused. This had to be some sort of trick. All this, just for skipping out on drugs, alcohol, and tobacco—something I planned on doing anyway? Dad sensed what I was thinking.

"Right now this might seem like an easy thing for you to do," he said. "But four years is a long time and you might find that it becomes more difficult. It's your decision."

"Sure, I'll do it," I said.

We shook hands on it. And I went outside to shoot a few more baskets.

Wow, that was easy, I thought. I had just gotten use of a car.

But my dad knew something I didn't ...

CHAPTER 5

SEEING PAST FRIDAY NIGHT

My dad knew that one of the hardest things for a teenager is *Seeing Past Friday Night* (the title of my first book on this subject). After all, he had once been a teenager.

As you know, high school can be fun, terrifying, exciting, agonizing, boring, exhilarating, confusing, joyful, and even a little bit scary.

Literally overnight, everything is in a heightened state of change. There is a lot of drama with a little bit of chaos tossed in.

PROJECTING PAST HIGH SCHOOL

With all of this happening, it is difficult to project forward and realize that life can get even *better* after high school. It's hard to know that phenomenal things happen in your twenties. Nobody in their twenties ever wishes they could live out high school all over again. But, few teens take the time to consider *anything* beyond the football game on Friday night.

My dad knew this, which is why he challenged me with his proposal. He knew there were suppliers who were intent on targeting me, my brothers, and my sisters for their own profit. He knew the suppliers were counting on the chaos that results from the collision of new freedoms with limited experience.

But, there was something my dad *did not* know when we shook hands and made our agreement ...

CHAPTER 6

AND HE'S MY FRIEND!

Surprisingly, saying no to drugs, alcohol, and tobacco was the easiest thing I ever did. In fact, it sort of became fun. Of course, I didn't let my dad know that (maybe because I thought it would become increasingly difficult to do—which it never really did).

Every time I was offered a beer (always free, by the way), it was a *no-contest* decision. The choice was a beer or use of a car.

Let's see ... can of beer, or car. Let's go with car.

Cigarettes or car. Again, the car wins out.

Pot or car. You get the picture.

But something happened that I never expected. At first, when I declined an offer for a beer or a cigarette, people would want to know why I was saying no.

"Well, here's the deal," I said. "If I don't smoke, or drink, my parents promise me the use of a car and some other incentives."

As you might imagine, most people thought I had a pretty good thing going on. But I will never forget the night a good friend of mine kind of surprised me.

"Hey Scan, how 'bout a beer?"

"Aw, no thanks man. I got that contract-thing going on with my parents."

"C'mon, have one anyway. What's the harm in just having one?" he replied.

"Then the bet's off. I lose the incentives." I said.

"How are they going to find out?" he asked.

I was taken aback that one of the nicest guys I knew, a good friend, was actually suggesting I break my pledge, lie to my folks, and still have them pay for the incentives. And all for a beer? Really?

"You gotta be kidding me," I said. "You'd probably be the first one to tell them!"

Over the next couple of years other friends would occasionally act the same way, and it really made me wonder why it mattered to them at all that I throw in with the crowd and have a beer (I didn't really care if *they* drank or not). I honestly never figured out why some of my friends pressed me on that.

But, I can tell you what ended up being an interesting side effect of *Just Saying No* ...

CHAPTER 7

THE POWER OF SAYING NO

I learned that the world did not end when I said no to a friend who offered me a beer, cigarette, or pot. The universe barely veered off its axis when I set myself apart from the rest of the group.

This taught me an important lesson that I might not otherwise have come to realize; I could stand up to a little bit of peer pressure and be a little different. Over time, something else happened that I didn't expect.

It gave me a quiet confidence.

There is no other way to explain it, but it got me thinking. If I could benefit from standing apart from the group in this small way, what *else* could I do?

By simply denying myself some relatively unimportant things and by resisting some peer pressure, life had become easier and more enjoyable.

There was power in saying no.

And the power was considerable. On top of having a car available to me all of the time:

- I avoided getting a DWI/DUI/OVI and never had to pay those attorney bills!
- I escaped a cigarette habit in high school, saving me big bucks!

- ○ I dodged being a slave to suppliers of drugs, alcohol, or tobacco.
- ○ High school ended up being an incredibly happy time for me, and
- ○ I felt like it enabled me to be a better friend to my classmates.

And my younger brother and sister benefitted too, as they followed my example. The benefits of *Just Saying No* were so powerful, it made me realize that, even if I didn't have a guide, I would do it anyway.

DO IT ANYWAY!

Nobody owes you *anything* for doing these things that you ought to be doing for your own benefit. So, if you can't find a guide, *do it anyway*!

Don't shortchange yourself from a successful future just because you didn't receive added incentives. Living a phenomenal life and being a hero to your siblings is incentive enough.

Always remember that the war on drugs, alcohol, and tobacco does not *end* with you; it *begins* with you.

Because, as you know, there truly is a *Great Paradox* at play here ...

CHAPTER 8

THE GREAT PARADOX

Only by self-imposing rational limitations on our behavior do we achieve true freedom and greatness.

If you want the freedom that comes from being as fit as you can be. That freedom liberates you to:

- Hike Diamond Head in Waikiki to watch the whales,
- Participate in Paralympic events,
- Bike in a peloton event, or
- Ski all day long in Vail, Colorado.

Only by saying no to cigarettes, for example, can you truly do those things *to the best of your ability*.

Performing at your best physically, intellectually, and spiritually is true freedom. It's flat-out liberating! Despite any of your challenges or limitations, being the best version of yourself is nothing less than heroic. It inspires everyone around you.

As every top-performing athlete knows, only by setting

rational boundaries on our behavior can we really have it all! To better illustrate this paradox, let's look at it in *the reverse*.

I KNOW I WASN'T SPEEDING.

A friend of mine was one of the funniest guys I ever met in high school. He had a carefree attitude that was contagious. It wasn't long before people were saying these things about him:

"That guy will say or do *anything*!"

"Did you hear what _____ did Saturday night?"

"He's hilarious. He doesn't care about nothin'!"

Does this describe anyone you know? There is something appealing about a person who goes about things in such a fearless, happy-go-lucky way. Unfortunately, for my friend, he started getting in trouble in little ways, like getting suspended from school for a couple of days.

I didn't really take particular notice until he was quietly kicked off the baseball team junior year. I knew how much he liked playing. A couple of months later, things got a bit more serious. One Friday night, while driving home, he was pulled over by the Highway Patrol.

"Sir, do you know why I just pulled you over?" the officer asked.

My friend answered, "No officer. I know I wasn't speeding."

"No sir, you were definitely not speeding. You were going 32 miles per hour. Unfortunately, the speed limit on this highway is 65. I'm going to have to ask you to step out of the car."

Suddenly, my friend, who was known for 'doing everything', really couldn't do anything. His life of carpe diem—with no limits and no boundaries—had left him with fewer options than any of the rest of us had. He couldn't play baseball, his car privileges were suspended along with his license, and his choices for college were dramatically changed. He spent countless hours working on weekends and in the summer, just to pay for huge legal bills. As you can imagine, he was not at all happy.

This **Great Paradox** doesn't end with high school. Just ask any professional athlete, entrepreneur, doctor, artist, teacher, physical therapist, or business owner of any kind, and they will tell you the same thing:

Sometimes life can be tough, but it becomes infinitely easier when we are a bit tough on ourselves.

Now is the time for you to be intentional. Determine the boundaries you want to set for yourself to achieve the goals that are really important to you. Signing the *Just Say No* Promise Agreement is a great start!

Happiness depends on self-discipline, and self-discipline depends on courage. Have the courage to *Just Say No*.

CHAPTER 9

INCENTIVES AND REWARDS
The *Just Say No* Promise Agreement

Let's face it, if you want a car, there is a good chance that you're going to have to go out and buy one. But, all is not lost! It's time to negotiate. Here are your 5 steps to earning rewards for *Just Saying No*:

Step 1: Show that you are willing to *earn* the rewards. Start from a position of strength and make a pledge that you are personally 100% committed to keeping.

Step 2: Decide who will be your guide(s). Consider parents, grandparents, aunts, and uncles. Spread the pledge and involve more than one guide. It will be easier for them to do, and easier for you to sell what you are proposing.

Step 3: Determine the rewards for success. This is not the time to be greedy or unrealistic. Keep the rewards reasonable and affordable for your guides. Limit the rewards to things that are truly important to you.

My nephew negotiated for a free gas card from his aunt and uncle, partial use of the family car from his parents, and an allowance from his grandparents! Because this agreement was successful, his younger brother got the same deal. When they signed the agreement, I told both of them the same thing, "This will be the easiest *job* you will ever have."

Compare it to the part-time job you could get loading trucks or working at the local grocery store that nets you $7.50 an hour after-tax. The alarm clock goes off at 8:00 a.m. on Saturday morning so that you can get ready to cut grass, answer phones, or flip burgers. Do you really want to go through all that to spend the money on car insurance and your cell phone, if you could instead find a willing guide to help you with those costs in return for simply *saying no*? It's a whole lot easier than cleaning wheels all day down at the car wash. Better yet, keep the agreement *and* the job. You will always have discretionary cash on hand!

Step 4: Clearly identify the penalty for failing to follow through on your promise. Basically, this is an easy one. It is forfeiture of any incentives or rewards. The *Just Say No* Promise Agreement is not intended to be partially kept. What good would that be for any guide?

Step 5: Put it in writing. Read the *Just Say No* Promise Agreement. Make any changes or additions, and be ready to explain it to your guides.

Step 6: Present it to your guides. Let the negotiations begin!

Step 7: Prepare to be your own guide. It is perfectly understandable if you are unable to find a guide who is willing or able to offer you incentives. Most parents and extended family members already have a lot of other financial obligations they need to tend to. But, don't shortchange yourself. Do it anyway! Be your own guide. Invest in yourself! Sign both lines of the agreement. (Or sign a Promise Agreement that does not include rewards.) You will still have an agreement that you have to live up to, and a great excuse to have for your peers.

Step 8: Sign it! Be good to your word. Make your signature mean something! In clear and simple terms, be the hero.

What a powerful day that will be—when you stand at graduation, knowing that you kept this pact with yourself and with your guides. Think about telling *that* story for the rest of your life!

Of course, there will be obstacles ...

CHAPTER 10

FREE SAMPLES AND OTHER SALES TACTICS

Suppliers know the statistics. If they are not able to get you as a customer between the ages of 14 and 18, then they'll probably lose you for good, as a lifelong customer. They also know that if they lose you as a customer, then the odds of them getting your brother or sister as a customer go down dramatically.

That's why they spend millions of dollars each year on free samples. Anyone who has spent years dealing with addiction will tell you that they never had to pay for their cigarettes, or drugs, or alcohol when they first started using. However, they eventually ended up paying thousands of dollars to chase their habits.

During World War II, many of the men and women of the greatest generation were supplied with *free* cigarettes, addicting many of the bravest heroes among us to a lifetime of emphysema, cancer, and heart disease. This was hardly a fitting tribute to these heroes. The cigarette suppliers should have kept their *free* samples.

For some reason, everyone underestimates the marketing savvy of suppliers, as if they just stumbled upon their success in generating hundreds of millions of dollars in profits each year. In reality, they are among the top industries in the world in terms of marketing, production, warehousing, distribution, franchising, and pricing.

Likewise, various illegal drug producers use some of the most talented chemists in the world to create drugs that are more enticing and more addictive. As you know, they even add attractive packaging to make their drugs look appealing to your younger brother or sister!

EARLY ADOPTERS

Suppliers use *early adopters* to introduce their product to a new user group; a new population. Early adopters are often described as people who are the first to engage in high-risk behavior and who are very influential among their peers. They are sometimes viewed as *cool* upper-class students. Oftentimes, they exhibit a bravado that masks an underlying sense of insecurity.

These early adopters frequently have big egos, but relatively low self-esteem. While they exude an attitude of excitement and adventure, they are often acting out against sadness or problems that they are experiencing at home. Because of their hip facade, however, they are able to influence more mainstream teens to use the product and then pass it along to their friends.

THE *NEGATIVE SALE*

Suppliers love to use the *negative sale* strategy, because it is particularly effective. This is where they say, "Oh you shouldn't try it anyway—you're not cool enough to drink." Or, "You're too young to smoke pot," as if sucking smoke into your lungs denotes a certain amount of age-maturity. Or, a popular negative-sale slogan is, "It's probably too dangerous for you." Don't allow yourself to be sucked into using *any* product by the negative sale.

DON'T UNDERESTIMATE THEM!

Don't underestimate their sophistication! They are the ones who approach you ten days after you have surgery for a sports injury to supply you with "replacement pain pills" because your doctor's prescription just expired. They are the ones who influence movie makers to place their products into motion pictures. They are the ones who are sometimes addicted themselves, and need to sell you drugs to fund their own habits.

Take them very seriously. Like *your-whole-life-depends-on-it* serious.

GET LOST!

Remember, if they don't get you, your brother, or your sister as customers by the time you are 18, they have probably lost you for good. So get lost, and make sure your siblings do too!

CHAPTER 11

HOW TO PREPARE FOR YOUR POLYGRAPH

I didn't know it at the time, but *saying no* also helped prepare me for my polygraph test.

Few people anticipate their polygraph test. If you want to become a police officer, or join one of the branches of the military; or think you might want to work for the C.I.A, F.B.I., Secret Service, or your local fire department, be prepared for this question:

"Have you ever engaged in the sale or purchase of illegal drugs?"

"Have you ever used drugs of any kind?"

"Have you ever committed a crime while under the influence of alcohol or drugs?"

They don't ask you if you have ever *been caught* doing these things!

Police officers can sometimes be forgiven for making a faulty decision, but they are never forgiven *if they lie* about what they did. Here's why. The results of their polygraph are of public record, and even the worst defense attorney will nullify any testimony the officer gives regarding the defendant. The attorney will say, "If they were willing to lie during their job interview to get their current position, how can we trust that they are telling us the truth now?" That is why police recruits who lie are not hired.

So prepare to either answer the questions honestly, or find another career. And if you are going for a job that requires you to travel in a car, or drive a boat, or fly a plane, get ready for:

"Have you ever operated a motorized vehicle while under the influence of drugs or alcohol?" Again, they don't care if you were ever *caught*.

AND DON'T FORGET YOUR FAVORITE FACEBOOK REVIEW!

I was having lunch with a group of social media experts, when a lady at our table mentioned that a new company had recently opened up in her hometown. After a lengthy hiring process, they prepared dozens of written job offers to various candidates.

Only afterwards did the company decide to search the candidate's Facebook pages. They were shocked to find that a third of their candidates exhibited behaviors that were completely contrary to the culture of their organization. Immediately, they sent out letters to 38 individuals, rescinding their employment offer.

Few of the 38 applicants who received the rejection letters (mostly young adults), ever learned the *real* reason for the company's change of heart.

AVOID BECOMING COLLATERAL DAMAGE

It is increasingly more difficult to conceal your behavior just by closely editing what *you* are in control of on social media, because your friends are also taking photos and posting comments about you. *Saying No* might help you avoid having to answer some potentially embarrassing questions.

So begin preparing for your polygraph and your first interview today!

CHAPTER 12

"What in the World Does Someone Like Me Have to Look Forward To?"

I asked myself this question when I was in high school. I had no idea what I wanted to do once my education came to an end. Who wants to work all the time anyway? I remember feeling intimidated by the idea of someday having to go out and find a job. Having to work *all day long* seemed like such a bummer, so boring, and you didn't even get to take summers off! What a drag that must be.

Maybe you've wondered the same thing from time to time. I remember thinking *what can I do, anyway? It's not like I have any extraordinary skills or anything*. But, that's where I was wrong.

YOU HAVE SUPER-POWERS PERFECTLY SUITED FOR A HEROIC FUTURE

Super-powers rarely apply to the things we like to do in high school. I had a variety of unique abilities, but I didn't notice them a whole lot because they didn't help me set any school track records, or get me a perfect score on the SAT. It wasn't until years later, when it came time to start a career that I discovered I had strengths that were perfectly suited to the field of investment real estate. In high school, I didn't even know what investment real estate *was*!

THE TEACHER

A friend of mine didn't know, until he was 20 years old, that he had an interest in teaching and coaching young adults. Recently, a high school in Cincinnati named their basketball gymnasium after him.

THE CHEF

It was two years after high school that another friend of mine discovered that he had great skills in the kitchen. He ended up travelling the world as a very popular chef.

THE LAW ENFORCEMENT GUY

Having a passion for keeping bullies from harming others isn't a typical trait that propels someone through high school. But it sure came in handy for my brother, a few years later, when he became one of the most highly decorated police officers in the country.

THE REAL ESTATE PERSON

A brilliant friend of mine continues to self-describe himself as having been one of the worst students in his high school class. Yet, he is now one of the most talented developers in Columbus, Ohio, who builds, owns, and operates hotels, office buildings, and athletic clubs.

THE RESTAURANT COUPLE

I remember asking a client of mine how he created one of the most popular restaurants in Columbus. He said, "I went to a banker-friend of mine and told him that I wanted to borrow money to open up a new restaurant. He looked at me and said, 'What in the world do you know about running a restaurant?' I said, 'Nothing. But I *do* know this. My wife, she makes the best lasagna I've ever had!'" Their restaurant soon became one of the most successful in town.

SOME GOOD NEWS! DEMOGRAPHICS ARE ON YOUR SIDE.

Recently, I asked a large group of young adults what kind of profession they were interested in. As you might guess, there was a wide variety of answers, including: Chef, Veterinarian, Teacher, Firefighter, Physical Therapist, Nurse, Graphic Designer, Filmmaker, Police Officer, Artist, Dog Trainer, Navy Pilot, Musician, Dentist, Writer, Social Worker, Welder, Architect, Oceanographer, Optometrist, and Flight Attendant.

I said, "Good for you. Because your timing is perfect! Your generation of teens is super-positioned to succeed," and pointed out that millions of new careers will open up as the baby boomers retire.

This is one of the reasons why, as great as high school is, you will never say, *I wish I could go back to high school*.

Nope! Not going to happen. High school is a wonderful time. When the time comes to graduate, you will be looking forward to moving on. Because *you're gonna love your twenties*!

Your future is not about all work and no play.

You want to:

- Fly to Chicago on the weekend for a Cubs game with your buddies?
- Spend 10 days vacationing in Europe?
- Mountain-bike through Zion National Park?
- Get involved with play troupes in your area?
- Volunteer to help at-risk children?
- Join the Peace Corps for a couple of years?
- Take up archery, or horseback riding, or fly fishing?
- Try your hand at writing a novel?

It's not all work. The fun and interesting stuff just gets started.

WHY ARE YOUR TWENTIES SO GREAT?

Because, in your twenties you have a lot of experience, combined with new freedoms, fueled by the dollars you earn in your career, topped off with a lot of youthful energy. It's really cool.

There are literally hundreds of examples I could give, of people who were absolutely clueless about what their future would be like, who are doing great and exciting things today. Sure, some of them are exceptional talents, where you could see their success coming from a mile away. But the vast majority of them are just ordinary people, like you and me, who began doing extraordinary things, once they came upon an idea or an opportunity they were passionate about; once they found their guitar ...

CHAPTER 13

FINDING YOUR GUITAR

My favorite songwriter is country music artist Brad Paisley, who grew up in the small town of Glen Dale, West Virginia. When Brad was very young, he received a guitar as a gift from his grandfather. It might have seemed like a simple gift at the time, but that guitar became a vehicle that helped propel Brad Paisley to become one of the most popular musical artists of all time.

I sometimes wonder what would have happened if he had never been given that guitar; or if he had instead been given a drum set or a saxophone.

We all need to find our own *guitars*, because ...

***Guitars* reveal your super-powers.**

Find a *guitar* that makes the most of your talents, skills, and abilities? For you, your *guitar* might be:

- A set of paint brushes,
- A writer's pen,
- A summer camp for young archeologists,
- A set of golf clubs,
- A biography of a great scientist,
- A fishing rod,

- A camera with black and white film,
- A set of hairstyling tools,
- A summer internship at a law firm,
- A summer job at a local zoo,
- A winter-workshop for aspiring journalists,
- A beekeeper's bonnet,
- A mallet and a chisel,
- An assignment as editor of the school newsletter,
- A book on gourmet cooking,
- A complete set of carpentry tools,
- A book on how to write jokes,
- A scuba outfit,
- A podcast microphone,
- A jigsaw and other woodworking tools,
- A gift of pilot lessons,
- A behind-the-set tour of a movie studio, or
- A chemistry set.

One of my wife's guitars was a sewing machine.

One Christmas morning, I surprised my wife with a brand-new Bernina sewing machine. A year later, she and her best friend opened a small business marketing the beautiful handmade purses and specialty items that they created.

Another one of her guitars was a tennis racquet. With that tennis racquet she joined a tennis team of people who have become some of her best friends. Oh, and she found out that she's really good at tennis!

FINDING YOUR GUITARS

The best way to find *guitars* that will propel you towards your goals and aspirations is to:

- **Take notice of other people's interests and professions.** Observe the interests of your friends, parents, teachers, coaches, extended family, etc. with the idea that some of *their* interests might also resonate with *you*.
- **Involve yourself with a wide variety of school activities.** High school is a great time to participate in the various activities of different groups. There, you might discover which activities match your passion and your talents.
- **Expose yourself to all kinds of different experiences:** Cooking, fencing, volunteering, acting, writing, surfing, painting, etc. The more the better!

Oh, and just because it's a guitar, don't rule out the possibility that your *guitar* might actually be a guitar! It was for Brad Paisley!

CHAPTER 14

THE TWO IMPOSTERS—
TRIUMPH AND DISASTER

The last day of school of my sophomore year, I was helping our history teacher straighten up the classroom. He also happened to be the varsity basketball coach. I had played on the freshman and junior-varsity teams that had compiled a 42-4 record. I was not one of the five starters on the team, but I loved playing basketball, and worked hard at it. Making the varsity team would be great, but I also knew that only six juniors and six seniors made the team each year.

As I was erasing the chalkboard, I said, "Coach, this summer I'm going to play basketball eight hours every day. When I come back next year, you're going to be amazed at how much better I am!"

He replied, "Scanlon, you're cut!"

Ouch.

Knowing how talented the other players were, I was not surprised by his reaction. As hard as I had worked at it, there were simply others who were taller, quicker, or better shooters than me. But it was still a big disappointment. I had been playing basketball all of my life (well, since seventh grade actually—but it *seemed* like forever). Now my career was at an end.

I didn't feel like I had been cut from the team, as much as I felt that the team had been cut out of my life. No more practices, games, or tournaments to look forward to with my buddies. And, it had been such a great way to stay in shape. Now what would I do? How would I fill the time?

I WAS NOT ALONE

Of course, I was not alone. All of my classmates, at one time or another, experienced major disappointments. Maybe they hadn't been selected as editor of the school paper, or voted onto student council. Some didn't get a role in the play that they wanted; others didn't 'letter' in their favorite sport. Disappointments also occurred when there was a breakup of a relationship, or when a fellow classmate relocated to another school.

HOW DO YOU MAKE YOURSELF FEEL OKAY WHEN DISAPPOINTMENTS HAPPEN TO *YOU*?

Honestly, I don't know. Nobody can really 'fix' that one for you. It's such a bummer. However, the Four A's might help you better *respond* to them:

Anticipate: Know in advance that *the disappointments are coming*. They are part of life and they *will* occur (especially in high school). Anticipating this will help you from feeling 'blindsided' by them. *Don't be shocked.*

Assess: See them for what they are. *Keep them in perspective.* They happen to everyone. *Realize that they will not last forever*.

Avoid: *Avoid any tendency to respond in a knee-jerk* way by turning to drugs or alcohol to 'dull the pain'. Think about it, *drugs and alcohol only makes things a whole lot worse*, **never** better.

Appreciate: This is hard to do when you are angry, upset, or frustrated by a setback. But *focus on the things for which you are most thankful*; a best friend, your family, your mountain bike, or violin, for example. Whatever they are, list them on a sheet of paper. *It is impossible to be completely sad and grateful at the same time.*

DEALING WITH DISAPPOINTMENT'S COUSIN— TRIUMPH!

Not only do you have to anticipate extreme disappointment, you also have to be careful of those times of extreme elation.

- You just won the volleyball championship.
- Or the play is over, and you and your classmates were the stars! After months of focused teamwork, it all came together, and you brought down the house!
- Or you just got accepted to West Point, Ohio State, or a top trade school.

Anticipate that there will be times when you are ecstatic. There will be a natural inclination to celebrate. That is when you have to focus, and remember that the celebration is fine; but not if it includes drugs or alcohol. Whatever you are overjoyed by, isn't as important as staying strong to your commitment.

Be careful of the two imposters, Triumph and Disaster. Remember, they are only temporary. Keep them in their proper perspective.

CHAPTER 15

"I Wish I Had Smoked More Cigarettes."

My promise to you is this.

Nobody ever looks back on their high school years and says:

- "I wish I had smoked more cigarettes. I'd be a pack-a-day smoker by now!"
- "I wish I had stayed out drinking until 2:00 a.m. more often."
- "I wish I had bought a bunch of drugs while in school."

They don't. And you won't either.

Some people use drugs, alcohol, or tobacco because they think they are going to miss out on something if they don't. They fear they will look back and regret that they didn't partake when they had the chance!

I absolutely promise you that you will never look back and feel as if you missed out on anything. Nobody looks back and wishes they had spent more days fighting off hangovers by sleeping in past noon.

Nobody enjoys the six months they spend working weekends to pay off the attorney they had to hire to defend their DUI (or any of the 'I's), or the $15,000 it costs for a one-month stay in a drug rehab facility.

And *you* will not either!

YOU ACTUALLY MISS OUT ON THE BAD STUFF!

If you confront the storm, you will not look back with serious regrets:

- Did you hurt someone?
- Did you waste a lot of time and money?
- Did you adversely influence the behavior of your brother or sister?
- Did you form an addiction that you have to overcome?
- Did it cost you a college acceptance or a career opportunity?
- Did you do a hundred things that you never intended to do?

Now is the time to write a letter to your future self ...

CHAPTER 16

A Letter to Your Future Self

"Do you ever wish you could travel back in time and have a conversation with your younger self?" That is what a friend of ours asked one day when a few of us were having lunch after playing a couple of sets of tennis. Everyone's answer was unanimous."

"Oh yeah."

Even writing a single letter with advice, back to our younger selves, could be hugely advantageous. Of course, until our quantum physicists figure out a way for us to do that, going back in time will remain impossible. But what about sending your *future* self a letter?

Seriously. Before all of the chaos and drama of high school sets in, why not send your future self a letter saying, "Just get us through these four years safely. We have a big life ahead of us, and most of it happens after high school. *Just Say No* for four short years and then we will take on the world!"

THE CALM BEFORE THE STORM.

Think about it. You're smart enough and mature enough right now to know what you should do. And, you have the advantage of being in the calm before the storm. Your future self might not have that calm.

THE *JUST SAY NO* PROMISE AGREEMENT IS THAT LETTER TO YOURSELF.

We value promises and the people who keep them. Think about the person in your life who you could confide in, knowing that you could trust their promise to keep the conversation confidential. Chances are, the person you just thought of, is one of your best friends or favorite relatives. A promise kept is a very special thing.

So, make a historic promise during the calm before the storm. Write yourself a letter, in the form of a Promise Agreement between you and your guide.

PAGE ONE OF YOUR DIARY?

Let the Promise Agreement serve as the first chapter of your life's story. (Maybe it would be cool to fold it up and put it in the front of the first page of your personal diary.) It is a tangible commitment to your big, heroic future.

Your future self with thank you!

THANK YOU!

Thank you for taking the time to read this book. I hope …

- You truly understand that, despite any limitations or challenges you have right now, you were designed to live a big life,
- You *always* dream heroic dreams,
- You realize that you have super powers that are perfectly suited for a heroic future.
- You act upon the premise of this book. That you write a letter to yourself in advance that says *keep me safe to fight another day; get me through these next four years safely. I have big things ahead of me*!
- You set a great example for any of your brothers and sisters.
- You remember that when life gets tough, making bad decisions with drugs, alcohol, and tobacco only make things worse. And by setting up rational boundaries you can make your life infinitely better.

But I mostly hope that your high school story has a victorious ending. That you make a promise, keep it, and then, upon a job well done, look your guide in the eye, shake their hand, and say *thank you*. *That* will be your greatest reward.

What a day that will be. Because, every story needs a hero!

Garrett K. Scanlon

www.JustSayNo.org

ABOUT THE AUTHOR

GARRETT K. SCANLON has served as a volunteer instructor, author, and speaker at middle schools, high schools, rotaries, business organizations, and parent events over the last 15 years.

Since his days as an award-winning Middle School Consultant for Junior Achievement, an experience he greatly recommends to others, Garrett has provided teens with unique concepts and *tangible* tools to help them thrive during their high school years.

Garrett is founder of JustSayNo.org, a website dedicated to helping teens partner with their parents, grandparents, aunts, and uncles to confront binge drinking, drug use, and smoking. The *Just Say No* Promise Agreement continues to inspire students to motivate themselves, months and years after Garrett has left their school.

He is also the author of *Walking and Talking—57 Stories of Success and Humor in the Real Estate World of Business*, Seeing Past Friday Night, *A Road to Bountiful*, and *Single Page Life Plan*.

Garrett is available to speak to school assemblies, parent groups, rotaries, podcast-venues, churches, and drug and alcohol prevention events of any kind.

To learn more, visit JustSayNo.org.

How to Bring JustSayNo.org to Your School, Parent Group, Church, Rotary, SADD/MADD Functions, Web Tribe, Red Ribbon Week, or Prevention Event!

Garrett Scanlon is available to tailor a *Just Say No* Presentation to your group or event. He will bring copies of his books and help your heroes and guides put together a personalized Promise Agreement today!

If you would like to:

- **Schedule** Garrett to speak to your organization,
- **Purchase** bulk-rate copies of *Just Say No*,
- **Subscribe** free to our blog,
- **Get involved** with the *Just Say No* Program,
- **Sponsor** schools to hear the *Just Say No* message,
- **Refer us to groups** who would benefit from *Just Say No*,
- **Donate added rewards** to encourage teens to *Just Say No*,
- **Download a free Promise Agreement**,
- **Provide us with ideas** on how we can improve our message,
- **Tell us your *Just Say No* story**,

Please visit: www.JustSayNo.org

The *Just Say No* Promise Agreement
(JustSayNo.org)

Terms and Conditions:

I, _____ (**Student**) hereby agree to the following promises, beginning today through August 10, 20___ (check all that apply):

- ❏ I will not consume any form of alcohol.
- ❏ I will not use drugs of any kind, in any form, in any way.
- ❏ I will not use tobacco products of any kind.
- ❏ I will not ride as a passenger in a car driven by any person who has consumed alcohol and/or drugs.
- ❏ In the event I find myself in a risky situation and in need of a ride, I will call the sponsor for a ride home.
- ❏ Other (if any): _____
  _____
  _____
  _____

I (We), _____
_____ (**Sponsor(s)**) hereby agree to the following (check any or all that apply):

- ❏ Provide Student with the personal use of a car on the following basis:
  _____
  _____
  _____
  _____
- ❏ Pay for _____% of Student's car insurance, except for any added insurance cost that results from Student being ticketed for a moving violation.
- ❏ Pay for _____% of Student's gasoline expense, not to exceed $_____ per month.
- ❏ Pay for _____% of Student's use of a cell phone, not to exceed $_____ per month.
- ❏ Other (if any): _____
  _____
  _____
  _____
  _____. (*Continued on next page, if checked here:* ❏)

Conditions of Termination: Neither party may take legal recourse of any kind against the other. Sponsor may terminate this agreement if it becomes financially untenable to the Sponsor. Student may not terminate this agreement. The intent of this promise is for it to be fully kept, not partially fulfilled. All parties agree to hold JustSayNo.org harmless, as stated below.*

Penalty for Violation of Terms and Conditions by Student: If Student violates *any* term of this agreement, Student agrees to immediately report the violation to Sponsor(s) who shall, at Sponsor's sole discretion, do any or all of the following:
1. Terminate this agreement making it null and void and of no effect.
2. Temporarily suspend the providing of the incentives stated above, for any time-period that is deemed appropriate by the Sponsor(s).

Further Acknowledgments: Student and Sponsor(s) enter this agreement fully aware of a.) There are many challenges and difficulties that Student will surely experience as a result of peer pressure and other high school pressures, and b.) There is considerable financial cost to Sponsor(s) to provide the incentives contained herein. Both parties enter into this agreement by free will, and without coercion. While there is no inherent obligation of any Sponsor to provide these incentive, Sponsor does so to help Student achieve lofty goals.

Entire Agreement:
No verbal terms or conditions are part of this agreement. This agreement represents the entire agreement. Any changes must be made in writing, and agreed upon by both parties.

Signed this _____ day of _____, 20_____

Student: _____

Sponsor: _____

Sponsor(s): _____

*****Hold Harmless.** Use of this Promise Agreement constitutes consent by all parties that they will fully defend, indemnify, and hold harmless Garrett Scanlon and Just Say No.org from any and all claims, lawsuits, demands, causes of action, liability, loss, damage and/or injury, of any kind whatsoever (including without limitation all claims for monetary loss, property damage, equitable relief, personal injury and/or wrongful death), whether brought by an individual or other entity, or imposed by a court of law or by administrative action of any federal, state, or local governmental body or agency, arising out of, in any way whatsoever, any acts, omissions, negligence, or willful misconduct on the part of Just Say No, Garrett Scanlon, owners, personnel, agents, contractors, or volunteers.

© Copyright 2017, Garrett Scanlon—JustSayNo.org

The *Just Say No* Promise Agreement
(JustSayNo.org)

Terms and Conditions:

I, _____ (**Student**) hereby agree to the following promises, beginning today through August 10, 20___ (check all that apply):

- ❏ I will not consume any form of alcohol.
- ❏ I will not use drugs of any kind, in any form, in any way.
- ❏ I will not use tobacco products of any kind.
- ❏ I will not ride as a passenger in a car driven by any person who has consumed alcohol and/or drugs.
- ❏ In the event I find myself in a risky situation and in need of a ride, I will call the Guide for a ride home.
- ❏ Other (if any): _____

_____
_____
_____
_____

I (We), _____
_____ (**Parents, Grandparents, Aunts, Uncles**) greatly respect student's decision to avoid drugs, alcohol, and tobacco during their high school years, and agree to:

- ❏ Provide transportation to Student in the event Student happens to be in an environment that is unsafe and needs a ride home.
- ❏ Offer encouragement, and requested guidance, as Student walks along this impressive and important path.
- ❏ Other (if any): _____

_____
_____
_____
_____
_____

Conditions of Termination: Neither party may take legal recourse of any kind against the other. The intent of this promise is for it to be fully kept, not partially fulfilled. All parties agree to hold JustSayNo.org harmless, as stated below.*

Penalty for Violation of Terms and Conditions by Student: If Student violates *any* term of this agreement, Student agrees to immediately report the violation to Guide(s).

Further Acknowledgments: Student and Guide(s) enter this agreement fully aware:

- There are many challenges and difficulties Student will surely experience as a result of peer pressure and other high school pressures, and
- Both parties enter into this agreement by free will, and without coercion.

Entire Agreement:
No verbal terms or conditions are part of this agreement. This agreement represents the entire agreement. Any changes must be made in writing, and agreed upon by both parties.

Signed this _____ day of _____, 20_____

Student: _____

Guide: _____

Guide(s): _____

*****Hold Harmless.** Use of this Promise Agreement constitutes consent by all parties that they will fully defend, indemnify, and hold harmless Garrett Scanlon and Just Say No.org from any and all claims, lawsuits, demands, causes of action, liability, loss, damage and/or injury, of any kind whatsoever (including without limitation all claims for monetary loss, property damage, equitable relief, personal injury and/or wrongful death), whether brought by an individual or other entity, or imposed by a court of law or by administrative action of any federal, state, or local governmental body or agency, arising out of, in any way whatsoever, any acts, omissions, negligence, or willful misconduct on the part of Just Say No, Garrett Scanlon, owners, personnel, agents, contractors, or volunteers.

© Copyright 2017, Garrett Scanlon—JustSayNo.org

www.ingramcontent.com/pod-product-compliance
Lightning Source LLC
LaVergne TN
LVHW051559080426
835510LV00020B/3047